BEYOND CUSTOMER SERVICE

Revised Edition

Richard F. Gerson, Ph.D.

50-Minute Manager™

This 50-Minute Manager™ book is designed to be an excellent workbook for self-study as well as classroom learning. All material is copyright-protected and cannot be duplicated without permission from the publisher. *Therefore, be sure to order a copy for every training participant through our Web site, 50minutemanager.com.*

BEYOND CUSTOMER SERVICE
Revised Edition

by
Richard F. Gerson, Ph.D.

CREDITS:

Managing Editor: **Kathleen Barcos**

Editor: **Kay Keppler**

VP, Product Development: **Charlie Blum**

Production Editor: **Genevieve McDermott**

Production Artist: **Nicole Phillips**

Trademarks
50-Minute Manager™ is a trademark of Logical Operations.

Some of the product names and company names used in this book have been used for identification purposes only and may be trademarks or registered trademarks of their respective manufacturers and sellers.

Disclaimer
We reserve the right to revise this publication and make changes from time to time in its content without notice.

ISBN 10: 1-56052-461-8
ISBN 13: 978-1-56052-461-8
Library of Congress Catalog Card Number 97-67632
Printed in the United States of America
11 12 13 11 10 09

LEARNING OJECTIVES FOR:

BEYOND CUSTOMER SERVICE
REVISED EDITION

The objectives for *Beyond Customer Service—Revised Edition* are listed below. They have been developed to guide the user to the core issues covered in this book.

THE OBJECTIVES OF THIS BOOK ARE TO HELP THE USER:

1) Learn how good customer service can expand beyond the immediate sale

2) Gain insights into the needs and expectations of customers

3) Find ways to retain customers through employee training and effective communication

4) Consider examples of quality customer service

ASSESSING PROGRESS

A 50-Minute Manager™ assessment is available for this book. The 25-item, multiple-choice and true/false questionnaire allows the reader to evaluate his or her comprehension of the subject matter.

To download the assessment and answer key, please visit *www.logicaloperations.com/file-downloads* and search by course title or part number.

Assessments should not be used in any employee selection process.

About the Author:

Richard F. Gerson, Ph.D. is president of Gerson Goodson, Inc., a relationship marketing and loyalty-building customer service consulting and training firm serving small businesses, entrepreneurs, Fortune 500 companies and other consultants. Dr. Gerson's marketing consultations have helped numerous businesses get started and be successful and he has helped several companies bring new products to market. He has developed unique training programs for marketing, customer service, communication, team building and personal training for peak performance. He is an expert in developing customer service programs and systems for businesses, then helping those businesses implement customer-focused retention and loyalty programs. He is also available as a speaker or trainer for your company or professional association. Dr. Gerson can be reached by writing or calling: Richard F. Gerson, Ph.D.

Gerson Goodson Performance Management

2451 McMullen Booth Road, Ste. 216

(727) 726-7619; (727) 726-2406 (FAX)

e-mail: getrich@richgerson.comwww.richgerson.com

CONTENTS

Dedication:

This book is dedicated to my wife Robbie and our sons Michael and Mitchell, who continue to teach me the true meaning of satisfaction in life.
Thank you all.

P A R T

I

Customer Service and Beyond

THE IMPORTANCE OF CUSTOMER SERVICE TO BUSINESS SUCCESS

Customer service is the critical factor for success in business. Your customer service must be better than your competitors' if your business is to attract and retain customers. Remember that the greatest profits result from customer retention, loyalty and repurchases rather than new customer acquisitions.

Much of customer service comes down to common sense. Give customers what they want and make sure they're happy. If you just manage complaints, offer refunds, or smile at customers, you are only providing a small part of excellent customer service. Customer service also means going out of your way for the customer, doing everything possible to satisfy the customer, and making decisions that benefit the customer, sometimes even at the expense of the business. (When this happens, consider the future potential of that customer's business for you.)

Now, I am not saying that you should give away the store to the customer. I am saying you must know when and how often the customer is right. When customers try to take advantage of you or become disruptive or abusive, they definitely are not right. While they may not always be right, *they are always the customer*. That's the only point you have to remember.

The Payoff of Superior Customer Service

Several years ago, you couldn't pay businesses to train their employees to provide good customer service. Some businesses thought that customers would come in, buy something, use it, and eventually leave the business anyway, so it really didn't matter if you were nice to them or not.

Can you believe that mindset in today's competitive environment?

Customer service pays. You may have to spend some dollars in training programs for your staff, and there may be other costs involved in revamping or revising your service delivery systems within your organization. Still, in the long run, customer service always pays off, and the way it pays off the most is in *long-term customer retention*.

THE IMPORTANCE OF CUSTOMER SERVICE TO BUSINESS SUCCESS (continued)

Common Sense Customer Service

High-quality customer service is as much a marketing tool for your business as it is a management approach or philosophy. Quality service motivates customers to tell others about you, and these referrals essentially create a customer sales force. The least expensive way to acquire new customers is through word-of-mouth referrals.

Good service also makes management easier because everybody is committed to the same goal. Employees are happier knowing they can do whatever it takes, without fear of reprisal or repercussions, to satisfy the customer. The results are increased satisfaction and referrals on the part of the customer, increased productivity from the employees, and increased profitability for the business.

The next few sections will provide you with a formula for calculating the costs of poor service, some startling service statistics, and information on the lifetime value and marginal net worth of a customer. If this information doesn't motivate you to provide the ultimate in customer service, then maybe you should think about what you'll be doing when your competitors steal your customers from you.

THE COST OF POOR CUSTOMER SERVICE

Customer service pays in many ways, including long-term customer retention and increased profitability. Many businesses understand the cost of acquiring a customer, but not the cost of losing one. In fact, it costs five to six times more to acquire a customer than it does to do business with a current customer.

Let's figure out how much it costs to lose a customer, using a formula based on information from the U.S. Office of Consumer Affairs. You need to know three figures to complete the formula: annual revenues, the number of customers you have, and the cost of acquiring and keeping them, including marketing, sales, advertising, discounts, etc. You can use dollar amounts or the percentage of sales to help in your calculations.

What You Lose

Let us assume that your hypothetical business has revenues of $10 million a year from 2,500 customers. We will also assume that the cost of sales is 66% of revenue, or $6.6 million. Now, plug these figures into the formula on page 7 and see what poor customer service really costs your company.

Take the total number of customers, and multiply it by 25% (an estimate for this example) to get the number of dissatisfied customers. Multiply that result by 70%, an estimate of the number of dissatisfied customers who will switch to a competitor. Divide total annual revenues by the number of customers to get the average revenue of one customer. Multiply this by the number who switched, and you get the cost of losing your customers.

Next, calculate your lost opportunity revenue by assuming each dissatisfied customer will tell 10 people. Assume that 2% of these will buy elsewhere. Multiply this number by the average revenue per customer and you get your potential lost revenue.

To determine your customer acquisition and replacement costs, multiply your total annual revenues by 66%, and divide that by your total number of customers to get your average cost per customer. Multiply this result by five to get your replacement cost per customer.

THE COST OF POOR CUSTOMER SERVICE (continued)

Now, add up all your results to get your total cost of poor service. Multiply that figure by 10 to determine the costs of poor service over a 10-year period, considered to be the customer's lifetime for doing business with you.

No business of any size can afford to lose and acquire customers continuously. These results should motivate you to improve your customer service programs so that they focus on long-term customer retention.

THE COST OF POOR SERVICE

Lost Customer Revenue

A. Annual revenue	$ 10,000,000
B. Total number of customers	2,500
C. Percentage of dissatisfied customers	× .25
D. Number of dissatisfied customers (C × B)	= 625
E. Percentage of dissatisfied customers who are likely to switch	× .70
F. Number of dissatisfied customers who will switch	= 437.5
G. Average revenue per customer (A ÷ B)	$ 4,000
H. Revenue lost through poor service (F × G)	$ (1,750,000)

Lost Opportunity Revenue

I. Number of other people dissatisfied customers tell (F × 10)	4,375
J. Number of potential customers who buy elsewhere due to negative word of mouth (assume one in 50 tell, therefore 1 × .02)	87.5
K. Potential lost revenue (J × G)	$ (350,000)

Customer Replacement Costs

L. Customer acquisition costs (66% × A)	$ 6,600,000
M. Average cost per customer (L ÷ B)	2,640
N. Replacement cost for lost customers (M × 5)	$ (13,200)

Total Costs

O. Total annual cost (H + K + N)	$ (2,113,200)
P. Total cost over customer's lifetime of doing business for 10 years (O × 10)	$ (21,132,000)

In this frightening example, the hypothetical company will lose more than $2 million a year due to poor service and low customer retention. Now fill in the chart on the next page for your company. Your results will probably motivate you to improve your customer service and retention efforts.

THE COST OF POOR SERVICE

Fill in this chart for your own company.

Lost Customer Revenue

A. Annual revenue $ _____

B. Total number of customers _____

C. Percentage of dissatisfied customers × .25

D. Number of dissatisfied customers (C × B) = _____

E. Percentage of dissatisfied customers who are likely to switch × .70

F. Number of dissatisfied customers who will switch = _____

G. Average revenue per customer (A ÷ B) $ _____

H. Revenue lost through poor service (F × G) $ _____

Lost Opportunity Revenue

I. Number of other people dissatisfied customers tell (F × 10) _____

J. Number of potential customers who buy elsewhere due to negative word of mouth (assume one in 50 tell, therefore 1 × .02) _____

K. Potential lost revenue (J × G) $ _____

Customer Replacement Costs

L. Customer acquisition costs (__% × A) $ _____

M. Average cost per customer (L ÷ B) $ _____

N. Replacement cost for lost customers (M × 5) $ _____

Total Costs

O. Total annual cost (H + K + N) $ _____

P. Total cost over customer's lifetime of doing business for 10 years (O × 10) $ _____

KEEPING YOUR CUSTOMERS

Customers today are better educated than ever before. They are more careful about their purchases and the dollars they spend. They want value for their money. They also want good service and are willing to pay for it. But who are these customers, and how do you know if they're happy?

Startling Service Statistics

These statistics were compiled from a variety of sources.

► Only 4% of customers ever complain. That means your business may never hear from 96% of its customers, and 91% of those just go away because they feel complaining will not do them any good. In fact, complainers are more likely to continue doing business with you than noncomplainers.

► For every complaint your business receives, there are 26 other customers with unresolved complaints or problems, and six of those customers have serious problems. These are people you probably will never hear from. These are also people who can tell you how to make your business better. Get their feedback any way you can.

► Most customers who complain to you (54%–70%) will do business with you again if you resolve their complaint. If they feel you acted quickly and to their satisfaction, then up to 95% of them will do business with you again, and they probably will refer other people to you.

► A dissatisfied customer will tell up to 10 people about it. Approximately 13% of those will tell up to 20 people about their problem. You cannot afford the advertising to overcome this negative word of mouth.

► Happy customers, or customers who have had their complaints resolved, will tell between three and five people about their positive experience. Therefore, you have to satisfy three to four customers for every one that is dissatisfied with you. It is very difficult in any business to work with a 4:1 ratio against you. Customer retention programs will enhance the value of your customer service efforts.

► It costs five to six times more to attract new customers than to keep old ones, even when you have to go back and renew contacts with former customers. Additionally, customer loyalty and the lifetime value of a customer can be worth up to 10 times as much as the price of a single purchase.

► Businesses that provide superior customer service and achieve customer loyalty can charge more, realize greater profits, increase their market share and have customers willingly pay more for their products simply because of the good service. In fact, you can gain an average of 6% a year in market share simply by providing good service: satisfying and keeping your customers.

► The lifetime value of a customer, or the amount of purchases that customer would make over 10 years, is worth more than the cost of your returning their purchase price of one item. For example, supermarkets may realize up to $5,000 a year from one family. That means $50,000 over 10 years. Is it worth it for them to provide refunds when the customer returns a purchase? Is it worth it to you to have the good will and positive word of mouth this type of retention service will bring you?

► Customer service is governed by the rule of 10s. If it costs $10,000 to get a new customer, it takes only 10 seconds to lose one, and 10 years to get over it or for the problem to be resolved. You must work to keep your customers.

► Customers stop doing business with you because:

  • 1% die

  • 3% move away

  • 5% seek alternatives or develop other business relationships

  • 9% begin doing business with the competition

  • 14% are dissatisfied with the product or service

  • 68% are upset with the treatment they have received

If you look at these percentages, you actually have some control over 96% of the reasons customers stop doing business with you. If you're a regional, national or international company, you can lessen the effect of 99% of these reasons.

10

WHAT CAN YOU DO?

Why might people stop doing business with you? Obviously poor service is one reason, but what others come to mind? After you write down a reason, describe what you would do to correct the problem.

Reasons to Stop Doing Business   *Solutions*

_____

_____

_____

_____

_____

_____

_____

_____

_____

_____

_____

_____

_____

_____

_____

These statistics and the chart that helped you calculate the cost of losing customers emphasize the importance of customer service and retention programs. It is no longer enough to say your company provides good customer service. Nor is it enough to train and empower your people to offer those service behaviors that will satisfy the customers.

It is only through customer retention programs that you will be able to maintain your market share and competitive edge, keep your customers, and remain profitable. You must go Beyond Customer Service to keep customers for life.

REASONS FOR POOR SERVICE

Ask any consumer why companies give poor service, and they'll tell you. Some problems are common to many businesses. Does your company have any unique service problems? How many of them apply to your organization?

- Uncaring employees

- Poor employee training

- Negative attitudes of employees toward customers

- Differences in perception between what businesses think customers want and what customers actually want

- Differences in perception between the product or service businesses think they provide and what customers think they receive

- Differences in perception between the way businesses think customers want to be treated and the way customers really want to be treated, or are actually treated

- No customer service philosophy within the company

- Poor handling and resolution of complaints

- Employees are not empowered to provide good service, take responsibility, and make decisions that will satisfy the customer

- Poor treatment of employees as customers

Shoppers are price conscious. They will switch brands or suppliers simply because one is cheaper than the other. You can prevent this by providing superior customer service and employing customer retention strategies. Make it hard for them to leave you. Establish a personal relationship with your customers so that you maintain their loyalty and they continue to do business with you.

Never take a customer for granted. Be grateful they have decided to do business with you and not a competitor. Work as hard as you possibly can to deliver more than they expect, and you will have gone a long way toward retaining your customers.

LIFETIME VALUE OF A CUSTOMER

It costs money to get a customer, and it also costs the business money when it loses a customer. By now, you should have completed the form "The Cost of Poor Service," which is essentially what your business will lose in revenues if you lose customers because of poor treatment.

An important figure for you to know is the cost of acquiring a customer and what that customer's lifetime value is to your business. It costs five or six times as much to acquire a new customer as it does to continue selling to and serving a current or former customer. Therefore, one quick way to look at acquisition costs is to multiply the lost revenue per customer that you calculated on the form by five.

Another way to do this is to track all your expenditures for marketing, advertising and promotion and divide that figure by the number of new customers each activity generates. This gives you a more accurate picture of your true acquisition costs. It also will enable you to calculate the lifetime value of your customer as well as that customer's marginal net worth, which is how much money you can spend to acquire that customer based on the profit you'll make from their repeat purchases over their lifetime with you.

Let me explain these concepts more clearly because they are powerful customer service and marketing tools. In fact, your understanding of the lifetime value/marginal net worth concept can help you grow your business faster than your competitors.

LIFETIME VALUE AND MARGINAL NET WORTH

Let's say that you track all your marketing expenditures and have determined that it costs you $100 to acquire one customer. You learn that each new customer spends $500 with you on his or her first purchase of your product or service, which gives you a gross profit of $400. Let's use 20% of gross revenue, or $100 as your overhead figure, which leaves you $300 net profit per customer for the first year's purchase.

Your data show that each customer makes three additional purchases from you per year, which total $1,500. So, each customer spends about $2,000 a year in your business. Your average satisfied customer stays with you for five years, so his or her lifetime value to you is $10,000 in gross revenue ($500 × 4 purchases a year × 5 years). Each customer's marginal net worth is the lifetime value minus the acquisition costs, or $9,900. Moreover, you make an additional $100 profit on each purchase because there are no new acquisition costs.

You can now decide how much more you're willing to spend to acquire a new customer. Before you were spending only $100 to get a new customer, but you can easily spend $300 (your net profit from the first sale) or even $500 (your gross revenue from the first sale) to get that customer because you know that this one customer will be worth $10,000 to you over five years, and most of it will be pure profit.

However, you must provide superior customer service to all customers to ensure that they keep coming back to you for those five years. If the service does not exceed their expectations, they'll take their business elsewhere.

Using the concepts of lifetime value and marginal net worth forces you to combine marketing with great customer service to get and keep customers for life. Customers who stay with you a long time buy from you repeatedly, plus they refer more people to you, so your new customer acquisition costs decrease even more.

CUSTOMER SERVICE: ONE, TWO, THREE

Poor customer service is expensive. Good customer service is invaluable, and you can achieve it in your company. Here are three things you must do.

1. Commit to providing superior customer service at all levels of your company.

2. Develop a customer service system that is easy for your customers to use. See the seven-step process that follows.

3. Design and implement customer retention programs that will maintain customer loyalty, thereby increasing the probability that your customers will refer new buyers to your business. Remember to use these retention programs as both primary and supplementary marketing tools.

SEVEN STEPS TO A SUCCESSFUL CUSTOMER SERVICE SYSTEM

Developing a successful customer service system can be one of the most rewarding goals you achieve for your company. Like most goals, it requires planning and work. Following these seven steps will place you ahead of your competition and start you on your way to successful customer retention.

STEP 1. TOTAL MANAGEMENT COMMITMENT

Customer service programs cannot succeed within a company unless top management is committed to the concept. It is up to the president, CEO or owner to develop a clear and concise service vision for the company. Then management must communicate that vision, in the company's service mission statement, to all employees. Use the space below to write your own vision or mission statement for customer service and retention.

_____

_____

_____

_____

STEP 2. GET TO KNOW YOUR CUSTOMERS

Not only must you get to know your customers intimately, you must also understand them totally. You need to know what they like about you, what they dislike, what they want changed, how they want it changed, what needs they have, what their expectations are, what motivates them to buy, what satisfies them and what you must do to maintain their loyalty. The most effective way to get this information is simply to ask for it.

Once you start to know your customers, you must continue to learn about them. Their needs change on a regular—even daily—basis and you must keep up with them. Make it a policy to call your customers at least once a month to find out how they are doing and what they need. While this shows them you are interested in providing good customer service, it also helps you develop effective customer retention programs because it tells your customers you are interested in them as people.

SEVEN STEPS TO A SUCCESSFUL CUSTOMER SERVICE (continued)

STEP 3. DEVELOP STANDARDS OF SERVICE QUALITY PERFORMANCE

Customer service is not as intangible a concept as you may think. Each business has specific business practices that could be improved. For example, how many times does the phone ring before someone answers it? How many call transfers does it take to find someone to answer the customer's question? How long does it take to process an order or ship a replacement? When standards are set for ordinary business practices, you can be assured of superior performance by your employees. Remember, what gets measured gets done.

STEP 4. HIRE, TRAIN AND COMPENSATE GOOD STAFF

Good customer service and effective customer retention programs can be provided only by competent, qualified people. Your service is only as professional as the people who deliver it. If you want your business to be good to people, hire good people.

Then train them to provide the ultimate in customer service and retention. Be sure they understand what your company's standards of service are. Compensate them well because they are the primary contact your customers have with your company and the reason people will continue to do business with you. Also, these people are your company in the eyes and minds of the customers.

Give your staff the authority to make decisions on the spot to satisfy customers. Remember that serving and retaining customers is one of the hardest jobs in a company. If people have that responsibility, they must also have the authority to decide what they can do for a customer.

STEP 5. REWARD SERVICE ACCOMPLISHMENTS

Always recognize, reward and reinforce superior performances. Provide financial and psychological rewards and incentives for your people. Recognize the small wins and accomplishments the same way you would applaud and dramatize the major wins.

You must also reward your customers for good customer behavior. They appreciate recognition the same way your employees do. Recognizing your customers will go a long way toward retaining them and having them refer new people to you.

STEP 6. STAY CLOSE TO YOUR CUSTOMERS

Always stay in touch with your customers. Conduct continuous research to learn from them. Ask them questions right after they make a purchase, send them surveys in the mail, run contests that require participation in a survey, hold focus groups to get perceptions and opinions of your business, call them on the telephone, develop a customer council to advise you on their needs, and do anything else you must do to stay close to your customers. Most important of all, LISTEN to them.

Your relationship with the customer actually begins after the purchase is made. This is when you must activate your retention programs, and this is when the customer will get to see how much you really care. Arrange all customer interactions so they are win-win situations for both of you. The result will be more loyal customers.

SEVEN STEPS TO A SUCCESSFUL CUSTOMER SERVICE (continued)

STEP 7. WORK TOWARD CONTINUOUS IMPROVEMENT

Even though you have designed friendly and accessible customer service systems, hired and trained the best people and gone out of your way to learn about and satisfy your customers needs, you must remember that no system, business or program is perfect. Therefore, you must continuously work to improve your customer service and retention programs.

Your attempts at continuous improvement will be viewed positively by the customers and your employees. They will see that you are trying to become even better than you already are. And when you become better, your service to them will also be better. The result is more satisfied customers, more business for you and your staff, and greater profits.

Customer service pays, it does not cost. You must constantly work to provide the best service at all times. Your only goal for being in business should be to satisfy your customers. Once this is done, the growth, expansion and profits will take care of themselves. Follow these seven steps to implementing a customer service system, and you will find that it will be easy for you to go beyond customer service.

P A R T

II

Know Your Customer

WHAT CUSTOMERS REALLY NEED, WANT AND EXPECT

Going beyond customer service and keeping customers for life does not mean just doing things right. You must also do the right things right at the right time, as defined by the customer.

You must know exactly what customers need from you, what they want as a result of doing business with you, and what they expect throughout your relationship with them. The only way to learn this is to ask them.

Too many businesses think they know exactly what customers want, so they go out and give it to them. Most of the time, however, businesses guess wrong; so they run into trouble or go out of business altogether.

You don't have to assume anything in business. All you have to do is ask your customers what they need, want, and expect from you and they'll be happy to tell you. If you don't have any customers yet because you are just starting out, ask the customers of competitors what they want in the way of great customer service. They'll be only too happy to tell you, and, once you find out, you'll have a competitive advantage that you can use.

Here is a list of 10 needs that all customers have in one capacity or another. This list is neither complete nor perfect for your particular business. You should modify it, add items to it, delete items from it, and adapt it to make it work for your business. Remember that this list is just a starting point. Customers need from you:

1. Help
2. Respect and recognition
3. Comfort, compassion and support
4. To be listened to with empathy
5. Satisfaction
6. Trust and trustworthiness
7. A friendly, smiling face
8. Understanding
9. To be made to feel important
10. A quality product or service at a fair price

WHAT CUSTOMERS REALLY NEED, WANT AND EXPECT (continued)

The preceeding list covers some of the things customers need from you. There may be other things they want in addition to these. If they confuse needs and wants, it's your job to ask for clarification.

Furthermore, customers define criteria for successful service performance by establishing expectations, which have nothing to do with you or what you're doing.

Let's say a customer expects you to call within two hours, and you call the next day. You've clearly not met their expectations. How will they feel?

Think about how you feel when you're waiting for a table in a restaurant. The maitre d' tells you it will be only 15 minutes, and you're still waiting 30 minutes later. Your expectations of wait time have not been met, and you have negative thoughts about this restaurant. Even when you're seated, you begin the evening with a negative attitude that affects your entire experience.

To determine your customers' expectations of you, you must ask them directly. There is a sample customer survey in Appendix B, or you can use interviews, focus groups, telephone surveys, or other types of questionnaires.*

DETERMINE HOW TO SATISFY CUSTOMERS

Questioning the customers will give you some insight into what they need, want, and expect of you. You must also ask yourself some questions about your business. Here are five questions that will help you determine how your customers perceive doing business with you. (Then go out and ask these same questions, or a variation of them, of your customer base.)

1. What result or benefit will customers receive from my business?

2. What is a customer's need level for my programs and services?

3. How important is my product or service to a particular customer based on the needs or wants the purchase satisfies?

4. What are the perceived costs and perceived risks the customer has about doing business with me?

5. What must I do to keep the customer's business?

Once you and your customers have answered these questions, you'll have a good idea of how to satisfy your customers. Of course, your best knowledge will come from asking them exactly what they expect of you.

It used to be that if you provided good customer service, customers would seek you out instead of your competitors. When most businesses improved their service, it could no longer be used as a differentiating factor to bring customers in the door. So businesses found other ways to enhance both the products they provided and the customer service that went along with them. This is called value-added service.

These days good, even great customer service, only lets you stay in the game. To be successful, and to keep customers for life, you've got to provide greater than great customer service. You've got to consistently exceed customers' expectations so they come away from each transaction saying, "Wow."

HOW TO GET TO THE WOW FACTOR

Customers will say "Wow" based on what you do for them that they never expected. To provide great customer service and to keep customers for life, you need to be aware of the following:

- ▶ Attitudes

- ▶ Behaviors

- ▶ Concerns

- ▶ Desires, wants and wishes

- ▶ Expectations and intentions

- ▶ Perceptions

- ▶ Physical state affecting mental state and vice versa

- ▶ Influencers, such as family and friends

- ▶ Your personal appearance

- ▶ Business appearance and environment

- ▶ Communication

- ▶ Availability and accessibility of staff

- ▶ Costs of doing business and providing service

Pay attention to as many items on the list as possible. When you do, you'll go a long way to creating the "Wow" factor in your business. Combine your knowledge of these items with many of the other recommendations in this book and your customers will really be shouting WOW every time they do business with you.

Now that you've increased your awareness about how to create the WOW factor, you've got to understand how customers will behave when they do business with you. Here are 10 behavior patterns you will encounter from customers. You can probably identify many more. Ask yourself what you must do to work with and satisfy each type of customer. More specifically, after you read each description, ask yourself, "How will I handle that type of customer?"

10 Types of Customers

1. **The Superior, Know-It-All Customer.** This persons knows your business better than you do and will not hesitate to tell you and anyone else who will listen. Most often, they will tell you what you're doing wrong, even when you do things right.

2. **The Resistive Customer.** No matter what you try to do for these people, they will resist your every effort to satisfy them. It's as if they enjoy making themselves and others miserable, or at least stressing people out.

3. **The Dependent Customer.** This customer is like a newborn infant that is totally dependent on a parent. This type of customer wants you to do everything and will not lift a finger to help him- or herself.

4. **The Hostile/Antagonistic Customer.** This customer loves to pick a fight or simply wants to stir things up. These customers are not having a bad day; they usually have a bad life and they take it out on everyone they meet. Be careful—this customer can become verbally and physically abusive.

5. **The Depressed Customer.** Nothing satisfies this customer, yet, you have to pity anyone who is always sad. If you decide to listen to this customer's problems, do not become their therapist.

6. **The Uncommunicative Customer.** It's hard to know how to satisfy someone when he or she doesn't tell you what you need to know. In this case, silence is deafening, and it could be deadly to your efforts at customer retention.

7. **The Talkative Customer.** These customers probably just want someone to listen to them, but their constant talking can become annoying. You must develop a way to quiet them down without insulting them, making them feel disrespected, or shattering their self-esteem.

HOW TO GET TO THE WOW FACTOR
(continued)

8.   **The Let-Others-Speak-For-Me Customer.**   This person won't say a word to you, but has friends and family act as the intermediary or messenger. This customer is also a follower, so be careful not to let him or her get influenced by another customer who is negative.

9.   **The Chronic Complainer.**   While these customers probably are a combination of several other types, they deserve separate mention. They buy, they complain and they return what they bought. Or they want a refund. Or they want an extension on their warranty. Or they just want to chew your head off. Whatever you do for them, they will never be happy with you or your business. In fact, the only time they're really ever happy is when they're complaining and making someone else's life miserable.

10.   **The Perfect Customer.**   Here is the person who buys from you and is so satisfied with the purchase that they go out and recommend you and refer your business to other customers. If and when this customer complains, it is to provide you with feedback so you can improve your service the next time. Find your perfect customers; ask them what they love about doing business with you; then ask them for referrals. Ask them to serve as advocates on behalf of your business to other customers. Sometimes a customer can resolve another customer's problem better than a staff person can, and this creation of "community" within the business will help your customer retention efforts.

There you have it. Ten types of customer behaviors to beware of and understand. Train yourself and your staff how to identify and handle each type. It's important for everyone to know what to do because customers are the lifeblood of your business. Regardless of their behavior patterns, find out how to meet and exceed their expectations. Do whatever it takes, within reason, to dazzle and delight them. When they do business with you, have them leave every time saying WOW.

MANAGING ANGRY CUSTOMERS

Every business has its share of upset or angry customers. Some businesses handle them well; others don't. The surprising fact is that it's very simple and easy to manage an angry customer.

The key is knowing how to do it. Plus, you must know what they need from you right at the moment they are angry and what they expect of you after that.

What should you do when a customer is angry?

You should listen carefully, calm the customer down, and find out what you must do to satisfy that customer. The following sections will help you get a better understanding of what the angry customer is thinking and feeling, what they could be upset about (it may have nothing to do with you, your business, or what they bought from you), what they want from you when they are upset, and a 10-step process to help you better manage your angry customers.

WHY CUSTOMERS MAY BE UPSET

Customers can be upset for many reasons, some professional and some personal. You can find out what is bothering customers by asking them. Here is a comprehensive list of why customers can be upset. Take a look at your business and see which of these items apply, and if any other reasons need to be added to the list. If you have employees, make sure you train them to be aware of these possibilities and how to handle the situations that arise.

10 Reasons Customers May Be Upset

1. They had to wait too long.

2. Their expectations were not met.

3. They feel helpless, powerless, frustrated or victimized.

4. They feel no one listens to them.

5. They were treated poorly or discourteously.

6. They were told to do something by a staff person and it was wrong.

7. They have personal prejudices against you or your staff.

8. They want to control or manipulate you by making a lot of noise.

9. They don't trust anyone in the business or they had their integrity questioned by a staff person.

10. Your staff person argued with them.

WHAT CUSTOMERS WANT FROM YOU WHEN THEY ARE ANGRY

Knowing what is upsetting your customer is very important. It is just as important to know what they want from you when they are angry. You already know that if they're upset and complaining about something, the thing they want most is to have their complaint resolved. Each situation is unique, and you must handle it as such.

On a personal level, customers who are angry and complaining want certain things from you. They want to be:

- Heard

- Understood

- Empathized with

- Respected, with their dignity and integrity maintained

- Valued

- Made to feel important, correct or intelligent

- Appreciated for their business

- Taken seriously

- Guaranteed immediate action

- Assured the problem will not happen again

- Compensated in some way

Put yourself in the customer's position. Remember what it's like when you're a customer and you get angry. How are you treated? How does that make you feel? What did you want that service provider to do differently? What would you have done differently if you were the service provider instead of the customer?

When responding to an angry customer, consider the process of service recovery. This process holds true for both managing angry customers and managing complaints. You must always do something that follows this process. It's very important to give customers what they need psychologically and behaviorally.

WHAT TO DO WHEN THE CUSTOMER IS ANGRY

Here is the 10-step process that you should follow whenever you encounter an angry customer. Remember that you have to go through the service recovery process in some form. You'll see how it comes into play here.

STEP #1 — *Don't argue.* Acknowledge the customer's right to be angry and upset.

STEP #2 — *Listen carefully.* Allow the customer to vent. Although it may seem like an eternity, give him or her from 30 seconds to two minutes of uninterrupted talk time. Most people can't sustain a high level of emotional anger for this long if you're just listening without interrupting. Use your active, reflective and empathic listening skills to encourage them to keep talking.

STEP #3 — *Apologize and use reflective communication skills.* Tell them you're sorry and restate the problem as you understand it. Let them know that you will do everything possible to help them out because you want them to get over their anger.

STEP #4 — *Empathize.* Let them know you understand the problem from their point of view and how they're feeling.

STEP #5 — *Ask questions.* Clarify the problem and the customer's interpretation of it. Make certain you understand the situation, from his or her perspective as well as yours. Asking questions keeps you from making a statement that the customer may perceive as placing the blame elsewhere or passing along the responsibility to resolve the issue.

STEP #6 — *Thank the customer.* Only a small portion of your customers complain, so treat every complaint as an opportunity for improvement. When someone helps you get better, thank them.

STEP #7
Make restitution. Explain exactly what you will do to resolve the issue for your customer. Only do this after he or she is calm. After you explain what you will do, make sure he or she understands what will be done and that your efforts will be acceptable.

STEP #8
Do what you promise. You must deliver on your promise of restitution. If you underpromise and overdeliver, the customer will love you for life. If you don't do what you promised, you will never get another chance.

STEP #9
Follow up. Angry customers may feel better when they leave you, but it's up to you to make certain their angry feelings don't resurface and return later. Call or write them to make certain they still feel good about what you did for them.

STEP #10
Give them something extra. Give them a discount on their next purchase, something for free, or anything you can think of to compensate them for their troubles. The important thing is that the customer believes that you've gone out of your way for them when they were angry and that you want them to be satisfied and loyal customers.

There's your 10-step process for diffusing an angry customer. The following service-related phrases can help your communication even more. (These phrases work well in any situation where a disagreement has occurred.)

"I agree with you that . . ."

"I appreciate that . . ." or *"I appreciate your . . ."*

"I respect that . . ." or *"I respect you for . . ."*

"I understand . . ."

"You're right . . ."

Using these agreement or bridge phrases will improve all aspects of your interpersonal communication.

OTHER TYPES OF DIFFICULT CUSTOMERS

You will run into all types of customers in your business, not just angry ones. The angry customers are the ones whom you'll remember most and who will probably give you the most trouble. However, there are other types of customers to consider. Of course, there will always be the perfect customer, and I'll let you add your own description of that person to the one I provide.

Remember: the customer may not always be right, but the customer is always the customer. Your job in serving these types of customers and managing them, especially the angry ones, is to resolve their problems quickly and to their satisfaction. The result will be increased customer satisfaction, loyalty and retention.

Seven Types of Difficult Customers and How to Manage Them (Plus the Perfect Customer)

► **THE ANGRY CUSTOMER**

- Listen.
- Don't argue. Avoid letting your emotions or the situation get to you.
- Show respect and treat the customer with dignity.
- Ask tactful questions to identify the root of the problem.
- Offer positive, constructive solutions.

► **THE IMPATIENT CUSTOMER**

- Respond quickly to requests.
- Get down to business immediately. Omit details unless the customer requests them.
- Reassure the customer you will take care of the situation completely, on time, and the job will be done right the first time.
- Make the customer feel important. (Do this for all customers all the time.)

► **THE CONFUSED CUSTOMER**

- Find out exactly what is causing the confusion.
- Use sincerity to gain trust.
- Keep explanations brief and to the point. Focus on one item at a time to prevent further confusion.
- Reassure the customer about the proper decision.
- Be patient and provide guidance and further reassurance.

► THE FRIGHTENED CUSTOMER

- Do whatever you can and must to alleviate the fear, once you know exactly what it is and what's causing it.
- Speak calmly and softly.
- Build trust with your sincere offers to help.
- Offer simple explanations.
- Reassure the customer that everything will be fine and that you'll stay with them until the fear subsides.

► THE INSULTED CUSTOMER

- Apologize.
- Be calm and brief.
- Reassure them in a positive manner.
- Listen as the customer talks out the situation.
- Follow up with full explanations as to your actions and resolutions.

► THE TALKATIVE CUSTOMER

- Listen.
- Be polite, yet firm.
- Apologize and explain your time constraints and your reasons for leaving the conversation.
- Focus on giving the customer what he or she wants.
- Tell the customer when you'll get back to him or her with a response.

► THE PERFECT CUSTOMER

- Brings his or her frequency card for every visit.
- Uses the business or facility appropriately and participates in add-on purchase programs.
- Refers new customers to the business.
- Makes suggestions for improvements but never really complains.
- Repurchases on a regular basis.

Now you know how to identify and manage angry customers and handle other types of difficult customers. Treat these people with care. The outcome of your tender handling can result in these customers being former customers, or being so satisfied with how you treated them that they stay with you for life.

The success of your business is in your hands when it comes to managing these types of customers. Do whatever is necessary, and train your staff to do the same.

P A R T

III

Customer Retention

WELL YES, MADAME... BUT WE **DID** REMOVE THE STAIN,

DEVELOPING CUSTOMER RETENTION PROGRAMS

Customer service does not exist in a vacuum and neither do customer retention programs. You need an overall structure or guiding focus to make them work. Consider marketing as that guiding principle, and create all your customer retention programs under your marketing umbrella. This will enable you to track and evaluate your efforts. Once you set up the programs within the marketing plan, you can use customer service as an effective yet inexpensive marketing tool.*

Many companies think of customer service as something they do after the fact. They view the process more as a complaint-handling system than a marketing technique. Complaint handling is only one small part of customer service. You must make the decision now to develop superior customer service and retention programs that are proactive, rather than reactive.

Proactive vs. Reactive Efforts

Customer service has two sides. Reactive customer service comes after the fact—after a customer has had a problem, a complaint, is dissatisfied or has had to bring something to the attention of a business. Proactive service begins even before the customer walks in the door. Your business is already prepared to do everything possible to satisfy and keep the customer.

DEVELOPING CUSTOMER RETENTION PROGRAMS (continued)

One of the best examples of proactive service is making the buying experience as easy as possible for the customer. Speed up the purchase process, decrease waiting times (people hate to wait), make your business a nice place to be. Many businesses, especially service businesses, do not have a tangible item to sell. Therefore, the office, the appearance of the facility or the people, is the only tangible item the customer sees. You must make it pleasant and appealing. People will continue to do business with you because they like the way you look and this makes them feel comfortable.

Proactive service and retention does wonders for a company's bottom line. Add to this some other retention-getters, such as thanking customers for coming in, thanking them for shopping even when they do not buy, and offering them additional information so that they can make a better purchase decision. You will find they will keep coming back to you simply because you created a pleasant atmosphere, made it a nice place for them to shop and made it easy for them to buy.

Think of some ways you can be proactive in the service you provide to customers. What can you do for them before it needs doing so that they will want to continue to do business with you? Write down ideas, then try to implement one idea a week. You will be pleasantly surprised at the results.

_____

_____

_____

_____

_____

_____

_____

_____

_____

_____

INTERNAL *AND* EXTERNAL SERVICE

Everybody thinks of customer service as something you do to or for those people who buy from you. Another group of customers also deserves good service, and that group is your staff. Everyone who works for you or with you is also a customer. You must provide your employees with the same type of superior service and retention efforts as you do the buyers of your products. You cannot expect employees to provide excellent customer service if they are not treated well by their employer.

Ask yourself another question and write the answer below. Then check it with the explanation that follows.

Whom do you work for?

_____

Your simplest, one-line answer should have been the customer. If you are an employer or a business owner, you work for the buying customer and your employee customer. If you are an employee, you work for the buying customer and the other people who depend upon your work. Basically, if you are not directly serving the buying customer, you better be working for someone who is.

Employees as Customers

Employees are customers, too. So are their families and your stockholders. You must work to serve and retain them. You already know the cost of poor service to a buying customer. Now, what does poor service to an employee cost? You must include:

- Lost salaries paid to employees who have left the company

- Recruitment and hiring costs of new employees

- Training costs for new employees

- Turnover as a percentage of sales and profits

- Negative image as a company with high turnover

Do you have any additional factors that may be figured into the cost of not retaining your employees?

INTERNAL AND EXTERNAL SERVICE
(continued)

Employee retention is simply a function of superior internal customer service. Recruit, hire and train the best people with the best people attitudes. Then, empower them to make decisions. Give them authority to go with the responsibility they have of serving the customer. Recognize and reward their accomplishments and achievements. Treat them as you would your best customers. You will see tremendous results, such as lower recruiting and replacement costs, because more people will stay with you longer. Plus these people will refer other people to work for you, so you do not have to spend additional money on recruiting. Above all, remember that if you serve your employees well, they will serve you and your customers well.

RETENTION THROUGH VALUE CHAINS

A chain is only as strong as its weakest link. As a business, you have suppliers and final customers, with employees in between. This is your value chain. Set it up so that every link is strong.

Treat your suppliers right. Order what you know they can deliver. Expect delivery within a reasonable amount of time. Pay your bills to them on time or early. Reward their loyalty with more business. Create enhanced value for them so they will continue to do business with you.

Treat your employees right. They deserve it and your customers deserve it.

Treat your customers right. Listen to them. Find out what they need, want and expect. Then give them everything and more. Exceed their expectations. Put more value in the chain. Let them know who your suppliers are and how well you treat your employees. This will make them comfortable and secure with you, and they will continue to do business with you.

Value Chain

Draw your own value chain below. A basic, three-link chain has been provided for you. Follow it or create your own. Then list the actions you can take to add more value to your customer interactions.

ACTIONS:

_____

_____

_____

_____

VALUE-ADDED SERVICE

Drawing the value chain is the first step to providing value-added service. Value-added service means giving the customers more than they expect. Sometimes you can charge more for value-added service, because customers will pay the added price just to receive the quality service.

An example of value-added service is the concept of the "baker's dozen": you pay for 12 items and receive 13. Some companies have extended this idea to give you 14 or 15 items for the price of 12. This is their attempt to compete by providing value-added service.

Perhaps an employee decides that customer satisfaction is more important than company policy. For example, companies have policies stating that refunds or exchanges will be made only with the original sales receipt and carton before 30 days. If you ever brought something back on the 31st day, or without the receipt, and had a company representative accept it from you, you received value-added service.

By doing this, the representative ensures that you will be a satisfied customer and that you will continue to do business with their company. On the other hand, if you brought the item back, were rudely treated and told that the policy forbids late exchanges, how would you feel? Would you do business with them again? Probably not.

To see how well you're doing with your customers, check with your competition to see what they are doing with value-added service enhancements. If they are doing something you like, adapt it and make it work for your company.

Use the chart below to help you.

Competitor's Service Policy	What I Like	How I Will Adapt It

Now let's see how you can introduce value-added enhancements to your business.

Fill in the chart below to help you provide value-added service as a customer retention tool. Write your current customer-service policies or programs in the left column and the ways you will add value to them in the right column. When you have completed the chart, describe how these new value-added service enhancements will help your business.

COMPANY POLICIES	VALUE-ADDED ENHANCEMENTS
1.	
2.	
3.	
4.	
5.	
6.	
7.	
8.	
9.	
10.	

These enhancements will help my business by:

1. _____

2. _____

3. _____

4. _____

5. _____

SERVICE ENHANCEMENTS

Value-added service can be expanded to include service enhancements, which are basically the services you already offer with some improvements.

For example, let us assume you are a car dealer who guarantees repair work for six months or the car is repaired again, free. A service enhancement to this policy would be to provide the owner with a loaner car while you work on their car. If it is the second or third time you are trying to fix the same problem, and the fault is yours, you can refund the money for the original repair just because your customer was inconvenienced by bringing the car back again.

Or you could give a free gift with a purchase. This creates the perception that people are getting more for their money. And you know how everyone likes to receive a bargain.

What other types of service enhancements can you provide? Maybe you can offer toll-free telephone numbers, free technical support and free service calls or replacement parts for products under guarantee or warranty. List your service enhancements and why they would interest your customers. Be very specific when you list the benefits, as these become excellent marketing and advertising messages.

Current Service	Service Enhancement	Benefit

CUSTOMER SERVICE MARKETING

Your business doesn't have to be on a seesaw of losing customers and seeking new ones. You can go beyond customer service, increase customer retention, and enhance your marketing efforts all at the same time. In fact, your customer retention policies double as excellent marketing approaches for your business.

Take the following quiz. Answer each question with a "yes" or "no." On a separate sheet of paper, describe why you do or do not perform any of the following activities.

Does your business engage in:

		Yes	No
1.	Frequent buyer programs	☐	☐
2.	Frequent referral programs	☐	☐
3.	Thank-you cards	☐	☐
4.	Newsletters/Personal letter of news	☐	☐
5.	Telephone recalls	☐	☐
6.	Customer reward and recognition programs	☐	☐
7.	Customer special events	☐	☐
8.	Strategic alliances or partnerships	☐	☐

These 8 ideas are all customer retention policies that are also good marketing strategies for your business. The more "no" answers you have, the more programs you must develop to retain your customers.

CUSTOMER SERVICE MARKETING
(continued)

1. FREQUENT BUYER PROGRAMS

Frequent buyer programs are similar to the airlines' frequent flyer programs. You are rewarding those customers who buy from you regularly. The rewards do not have to be expensive or lavish. They just have to show the customer you appreciate their business. Be sure it is easy for all your regular customers to benefit from this program.

Consider a retail store that punches a card every time you buy something. After your tenth or twelfth purchase, you get something for free or at a significant discount. This policy encourages you to go back to shop there because you will receive a special reward when you meet a specific criterion. Repeat purchase cards are an excellent way to retain customers, and they are an excellent marketing tool, as well.

2. FREQUENT REFERRAL PROGRAMS

If your business depends on referrals, you should reward the people making referrals to you. Your rewards will also reinforce their behavior, thereby creating a positive cycle and a mutually beneficial relationship.

The best way to use a frequent referral reward program is to develop it in tiers, or levels. Here are some suggestions for rewards based on the number of referrals from one source. Don't forget to fill in how you would reinforce this behavior. Also, feel free to change the reward recommendation to suit your business or situation.

Number of Referrals	Reward Recommendation	My Reward
1	Thank you card	
2	Telephone call	
3	Flowers	
4	Small gift (under $10)	
5	Gift certificate (dinner for two)	

When the same person refers more than five people, do something special for that person. Then start the referral reward program all over again.

If your customers don't mind having their names visible in your store or office, create a referral bulletin board. Post the names of your current customers who refer new customers to you on this board each month, including the number of referrals they have made. People usually like to see their name written on something, and this will give them the satisfaction of knowing you appreciate their efforts. Also, it may create a healthy competition among your customers to see who can refer more new people to you each month. They benefit because you will reward and reinforce them, and you benefit from the new business and positive word of mouth.

Create a new customer welcome bulletin board. List the names of your new customers each month. This is the first step in a proactive customer retention program. When people see that you care enough to put their name up for everyone else to see, they will go out of their way to help you in your business and to remain loyal to you.

3. THANK-YOU CARDS

A simple and effective customer retention technique that few businesses exploit, writing a thank-you card and sending it to someone who has bought something from you, takes only a little extra effort. Cards are the best postage-stamp marketing investment you can make.

If you do not want to write out a card for every customer that purchases, then have your cards preprinted with a message that shows your appreciation. It is even more effective if you develop part of your customer-retention program around a series of these cards.

THANK YOU CARDS (continued)

Displayed are samples of preprinted cards that I have used for my customers. You can make them up at your local printer or purchase them from a specialty dealer. The cards are sent out in the order you see them: "Thank you for your business"; "Our customers are number 1"; and when the job is completed, "It was a pleasure working with you." When my company receives a referral, we send out the referral thank you card. All this information and the dates the cards are sent are tracked through our customer database.

Front

Inside

*W*e value your business highly and hope to be of service to you many times in the future.

Company Name Here

Front

Inside

We appreciate
your business and thank
you for the opportunity
of serving you!
You can always count
on our support!

Company Name Here

Front

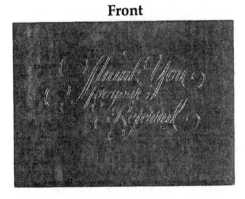

Inside

*H*ope we get the
opportunity to do it again
in the near future.

Company Name Here

Front

Inside

*Y*our confidence in us
is greatly appreciated.

Company Name Here

4. NEWSLETTERS/PERSONAL LETTER OF NEWS

Newsletters are a great way to keep your customers informed of what is going on in your business. You can tell them whatever information you need for them to know. And, because it is coming from you free of charge, they will be only too glad to read it.

One way to keep your customers involved with your business is to promote contests or other activities in the newsletter. Specify that they come to your store or office to win the contest. This is another good time to solidify their loyalty and make sure you retain them as customers.

One variation of the newsletter is a letter of news. Write a personal letter to each customer (using a computerized customer database makes this task very easy) and mention all the items you would have mentioned in a newsletter. Your customers will be pleased that you took the time to write them a personal letter. Here is an example of a one- to two-page letter of news:

SAMPLE—PERSONAL LETTER

Today's Date

Michael Mitchell
Any House
Anytown, USA

Dear Michael Mitchell:

I just wanted to thank you for continuing to do business with us. I also wanted to take this opportunity to tell you about some of the great things that are happening in our business and how they can benefit you. As you know, we have provided both marketing consulting and training services for you in the past year. Your comments indicated you were very satisfied and are interested in working with us again. Here is some exciting news to help you decide on when we can begin these programs.

New Marketing Book Gets Published

I have recently had the honor of having a marketing book published by Crisp Publications. It is called *Marketing Strategies for Small Business.* The book sells for $15.95. It is available to all our marketing consulting clients free of charge. If you participate in one of our marketing workshops, it is given to you as part of the workshop fee. It also reduces the cost of the workshop to you, since now there is no materials charge.

Corporate Videos Being Filmed

Several large corporations have asked us to film their presentations to prospective clients to be used for future training. Our videos are professionally done using state-of-the-art equipment. They can be as long as you need to get your message across. We provide all the necessary services, including script writing, filming, editing, sound, pre- and post-production.

The Last Training Seminar You Will Ever Need

It has taken more than 20 years of research in psychology, human behavior, human relations and communications. Now we have designed a training program that can help you achieve greater personal and professional success, more sales, more friendships, deeper and more meaningful relationships and a better love life. It is called *Persuasive Communication Skills,* and it teaches you about people's behavioral and interpersonal styles, sensory perceptual communication styles and the basic principles of effective human relations. The program is customized to suit your needs and budget.

I hope this information has been helpful to you. Please feel free to call me at (813) 726-7619 if you have any questions. Or, just stop by to say hello. We appreciate you as our customer, and we look forward to continuing our relationship with you.

Sincerely,

Richard F. Gerson, Ph.D.
President

5. TELEPHONE RECALLS

Telephone recalls work well in any type of business. If you are in a service business where customers need to make appointments, you can call them a day in advance to remind them of the appointment. Or, if they have not been in to see you in some time, you can call them to see how they are doing and to inform them of a reason to come in now to do business with you.

If your business is retail, you can personally call customers and invite them in for a special sale. This is often done by department stores who send mailers to their credit card holders inviting them to a sale before the general public is invited. If this makes you feel special, think how much more special you will feel when someone calls you personally.

When you are not able to make all the calls personally, write out a basic script for the caller. You want your message of caring for the customer to come across loud and clear.

When your customers call you, treat them with courtesy. Answer the phone in the following way: "Good (morning, afternoon), (company name), this is (your name). How may I help you?"

Never put a caller on hold for more than 30 seconds without coming back and telling them what the delay is. People hate to wait, and they will hang up and take their business elsewhere. If your customers complain that they cannot get through to you on the telephone, it may be time to install more telephone lines.

Some businesses use the telephone as their life's blood. Do not make the mistake of neglecting the telephone as a way to retain your customers. Call them regularly, even if it is just to say hello.

6. CUSTOMER REWARD & RECOGNITION PROGRAMS

Recognizing and rewarding your customers should be a regular business practice. Sending thank you cards tells customers you recognize their importance to your business. Giving them gifts for referrals shows them how much you appreciate their efforts on your behalf. Offering them rewards for making repeat purchases informs them you understand their contribution to your business success. But you can do more to retain customers.

First, recognize every customer that does business with you. Learn and use their names. If you cannot remember someone's name, at least acknowledge that you recognize that person as a regular customer. If someone is a new customer, go out of your way to learn their name and everything you can about them. They will appreciate your interest in them.

Next, make your customers feel important. Many businesses say they do this, but it is just not so. You have to give extra effort to make customers feel important, and once you do, you will keep them for life.

What are some ways you can make them feel important? Try these suggestions:

- Ask them about their family, especially their children or grandchildren.

- Congratulate them on some achievement or a job promotion.

- Ask for their advice on something related to your business.

- Tell them they look nice.

- Give them a surprise just for doing business with you.

You can probably think of several more ways to make people feel important. The key is to do this in a natural manner so that each individual customer feels and believes you are taking a special and sincere interest in him or her.

You can recognize and reward your customers in other ways. Invite your customers to special sales or give them special treatment. Hold a contest for your best customers and give the winner a trip as a grand prize. Give other winners gift certificates or dinners at fine restaurants. Print up VIP cards for your best customers that entitle them to extra discounts.

All these ideas are strictly customer retention ideas—they have nothing to do with serving the customer during the time of a purchase. Yet they are vitally important to the success of your business because they create added value for the customer.

It is very easy for a competitor to price merchandise the same as you do, to give the same type of guarantees as you do, and to provide the same extensive and courteous service as you do. If that happens, the only thing that will make a customer choose to do business with you is the value-added service you provide.

The chart on the following page will help you create your own customer recognition and reward program. Use the first column to describe the customer's action, the second to show that you recognize that behavior of the customer, the third to explain how you will reward that behavior. Remember, it is better to create a shorter list and do those things extremely well than to try to do many things only adequately.

RECOGNITION AND REWARD PROGRAM (continued)

Customer Action	How Recognized	How Rewarded
Samples:		
First Referral	Thank you note	Small discount
Second Referral	Telephone call	Box of candy
High Volume purchase	Telephone call	Dinner
_____	_____	_____
_____	_____	_____
_____	_____	_____

Employee Recognition and Reward Programs

Any customer retention program must include recognition and rewards for your employees. Remember that they are your customers, too, and on some occasions, they are your most important customers. Show them you care about them as much as you do about the external customers. Create a recognition and reward program for your employees just as you did for your customers in the last section.

When you treat employees as customers, their morale will improve, and they will want to do well for the company. Furthermore, they will want to continue working for you. Customers like to see the same faces all the time. Both your customers and your employees will enjoy the stability. People like doing business with people they know and like. Long-term employees provide that for you with your customers. Therefore, never forget or neglect your employees. Always treat them as customers. It is as important to retain them as it is to retain your external customers.

7. CUSTOMER SPECIAL EVENTS

Special events for your special customers are a great way to strengthen the relationship. Many companies have special sales for the general public while others have private sales for their credit card holders. You, too, can create a special event for your best customers.

Host a cocktail party or other social gathering at your place of business after hours. Invite several good customers to dinner at a nice restaurant. Treat them to a round of golf, tickets to a sporting event or show, or do something special for their families.

Special events for special people do not have to be elaborate or expensive. They only have to be special. Ask your customers what is important and special to them. Then, wait a short while and give them what they want and like. They will reward you with their loyalty.

8. STRATEGIC ALLIANCES AND PARTNERSHIPS

You would keep more of your customers if you made more of them your partners. This is not as crazy an idea as it may seem at first. You do not have to make your customers financial partners in your business. Rather, you make them partners in doing business. Here are a few suggestions.

Site Visits

Invite your customers to spend a day with you at your place of business. Let them go anywhere they please, ask questions of anyone, and even try to work for a while. Ask them to view everything with a critical eye.

Having them on site can be of tremendous benefit to you. First, it shows them you care enough to invite them into your business. Second, it tells them you think they are important, because you are asking their opinion on how to improve your business. Third, it helps you get an objective opinion from an outsider on how well your business is running.

After you invite customers on site, the next step in creating the strategic partnership is for you to visit your customers. This may be at their place of business, at their homes (depending on how close you have become with them) or at a social function. If you want to make a customer a strategic partner, you must become intimately involved with them. You must also offer to help them, just as they are helping you.

This idea of strategic partners may not be as new to you as you may think. Don't you work with one accountant? Do you have a personal physician? How many financial planners or stock brokers are you working with? How many suppliers are you working with? How long have you been working with these people?

All these relationships are strategic partnerships. You are helping these people succeed just as they are helping you succeed. Why shouldn't you do the same thing with your customers? Remember that it is easier and less expensive to do business with a current customer than to acquire a new one. And you will have more current customers if you create more strategic partnerships.

Customer as Sales Agent

Customers who perceive themselves as strategic partners for your business become your best sales agents. They will tell others about how great it is to do business with you. These new customers will come to you with a positive attitude because you have already been endorsed by someone they trust. It is up to you not to let the new customers down.

On the other hand, customers who are not your strategic partners may not say anything good about you. They may not say anything bad, in fact they may not say anything. No reference means no sale for you.

Therefore, try to make every customer a strategic partner. They can help you more than you know. And, even if there is someone who does not become your customer today, plant the seed for a strategic partnership in the future. You will be glad you did.

SERVICE RECOVERY: ANOTHER LOOK

Not all customers are happy customers. Sometimes you have to make up for bad service or a bad product. Service recovery means actions that tell the customer you will take care of their problem. Restitution is what you give your customers to compensate them for their inconvenience. You should welcome any situation that requires service recovery and restitution.

Complaints do not have to be loud or demanding. They can be very quiet and sometimes almost go unnoticed. Reread the startling service statistics and compare the number of people who don't complain with those who do. If someone complains, they are taking the time to help you improve your business. You, then, must take the time to acknowledge and resolve their complaints.

Every business or organization will have to face the fact that sometime, some customer will be unhappy, dissatisfied or upset with their product or service. It is your responsibility to resolve the problem as quickly as possible to the customer's satisfaction.

You probably already have some type of recovery and restitution program in place. Use the chart below to outline your program. Fill in the spaces in each column. Then read on to see if your program does all it could do.

Policy	Procedures	Exceptions (?)	Recovery/ Restitution
Returns	30 days w/ receipt	(Fill in here)	Exchange Product

SATISFYING UNHAPPY CUSTOMERS

Customers who complain feel annoyed, cheated or victimized. They also feel that their situation is the most important in the world. Understand these feelings and treat your customers accordingly. Dissatisfied customers tell up to 20 friends that they are unhappy with the way you do business. However, if you resolve their problems, 50%–74% of these same customers will do business with you again. Adapt the following five-step recovery program to your business and specific situation, and then train your employees to be sure it's implemented. Or, you can use the expanded 10-step process mentioned earlier in the book.

Service Recovery Program

1. Apologize.

First and foremost, say you are sorry for the inconvenience the customer has experienced. Be sincere—the customer will notice if you are not. A sincere apology usually defuses the customer's anger. Also, you must personally accept responsibility for the problem occurring and its resolution.

2. Urgent restatement.

Restate the problem as the customer described it to you to make certain you understand exactly what the customer means. Then, tell (and show, if possible) the customer that you will do everything possible to solve the problem and resolve the complaint immediately. Even if you can't resolve the problem to their fullest satisfaction, the customer will perceive that you were sincere and definitely intended to help. Their dissatisfaction will diminish.

3. Empathy.

Make certain you communicate clearly to your customers so that they understand that you know how they feel. Do not patronize or try to pacify them. Just show them and tell them you understand how they feel. Use phrases such as: "I understand," "I know how you feel," "I can see why you're upset."

SATISFYING UNHAPPY CUSTOMERS
(continued)

4. Restitution.

Here is your chance to make points. Not only will you take immediate action to resolve your customers' complaints, such as refunding their money, making an exchange or offering a credit, you will go a step further. Tell and show your customers you will make it up to them in some special way. You may have to provide them with a free gift for their troubles, or you may have to allow them to purchase a new item at a sale price. Whatever you do, look at it as adding value rather than spending extra money.

5. Follow up.

This is where most programs fail. Be sure to find out if your customer is satisfied. You can ask a simple question or two at the end of the recovery process: "Have we resolved your complaint to your satisfaction? What else may we do for you?" Then wait a few days and call the customer to make certain they are still satisfied. You can also send them a letter. A nice touch would be to enclose a coupon or gift certificate with the letter. Going the extra mile will help you create and keep a loyal customer. Also, keep track of what you did and said as well as how the customer responded. This will help you the next time the customer does business with you.

Use this basic five-step approach to service recovery and restitution as a guide to develop a workable program for your business. You may want to break the restitution step down into resolution (the action taken to resolve the complaint) and restitution (anything else that you do for the customer to compensate them for their inconvenience). Whatever you do, this program will also help you to consider service recovery and restitution as part of a larger complaint management program.

MANAGING COMPLAINTS FOR RETENTION AND SALES

This basic approach for handling a complaint and keeping a customer is also a unique sales opportunity. A customer is more motivated to buy from you right at the time you have taken special care of them (resolved their complaint) than at any other time. Once you have resolved the complaint to their satisfaction, you can begin working on a new sale. Use the 10 suggestions on turning customer complaints into additional sales to create loyal and long-term customers for your business.

Turn Customer Complaints into Sales

1. Understand why the customer is complaining. Most probably, a need has not been satisfied or an expectation has not been met.

2. Listen attentively. The customer wants your undivided attention and respect concerning this problem, and he or she deserves to get it.

3. Handle one complaint at a time, even if the customer has several. You can manage a single complaint most effectively and have a better chance of turning that complaint into a sale rather than trying to handle two or three complaints at once.

4. Ask the customer what the needs were at the time of purchase and why those needs are not now being met. Find out how the current needs differ from the original, and why the change occurred.

5. Tell the customer that you understand the complaint and that you are sorry there is a problem. Assure the customer that you will do everything possible to resolve the complaint immediately.

6. Once you have resolved the complaint, discuss new sales offers and their benefits.

7. Handle any objections you may receive to the new sales offer, and continue to manage the original complaint if it comes up again.

8. Attempt to close the new sale resulting from the customer complaint as if it were an original sale. Sometimes, these "complaint sales" are easier because the customer has already made a purchase and knows how your product or service can satisfy a need.

9. If you cannot resolve the complaint to the customer's satisfaction, offer alternatives such as speaking to a person of higher authority, exchanging the merchandise, or refunding their money.

10. More than 75% of the people who complain and have that complaint resolved immediately will make another purchase. Use this statistic to your advantage as you continue to try to close the "complaining" customer.

HOW TO C.A.R.E. FOR YOUR CUSTOMERS

To create loyal customers, you must show them that you CARE. If you CARE, your customers will reward you with their loyalty. To CARE properly for your customers, you must be:

Credible. Your reputation is all you have in the business world. Customers must believe in your product or service, your customer service policies, and your performance efforts. If they don't believe in you, they won't buy from you. Customers buy for five reasons: to save or make money, to improve their health, to save time, to feel secure or to boost their egos. If you promise that your product or service will do any of these five things for your customers, then it better perform. If it doesn't, you must implement your service recovery program to ensure their satisfaction and loyalty.

Accessible. Customers want to be able to access your customer service system quickly and easily. Don't make it difficult for them by passing them from employee to employee. Be accessible and customer friendly.

Reliable. Do what you say you will do at the time you say you will do it. Get it right the first time, get it done for the customer on time, and then check with the customer to ensure satisfaction. Reliability comes from the consistency in the performance of your product or service and the consistency with which you treat customers. When you are reliable, customers know what to expect from you and they like doing business with you.

Excellence. Customers believe that they themselves are important, and they want to do business with excellent companies and people. Provide excellent customer service and you will have excellent customer retention. Provide excellent training programs for your staff and you will have excellent performers who will ensure retention of your customers. If your work isn't excellent, it isn't good enough. Your customers want excellence and so should you.

Retaining your customers must become part of your regular business life. Follow the basic steps for recovery and restitution, manage complaints so that you can turn them into additional sales, and CARE for the customer. If you do, you will keep your customers for a long time.

RETENTION THROUGH TRAINING

Untrained employees present a bad image for your company. If your workers understand your product or service but cannot speak and listen to customers, you will not be in business very long. If your customers don't get the attention they deserve, they will take their business elsewhere.

Employee training is frequently an underutilized and underdeveloped method of customer retention. Most companies train their employees to do their jobs but not how to interact with customers. Both are equally important.

Recent statistics estimate that if a company spends 2%–5% of its annual payroll on employee training, it should realize about a 10% increase in net profit. Furthermore, companies with superior customer service and a loyal customer base can charge up to 10% more than their competitors. So if you train your employees to provide superior customer service, your net profit can increase by 20%.

Types of Training Programs

You can provide many types of training programs for your employees. The most important programs for customer retention are:

- Customer service: company policies, systems and procedures

- Team building: developing cohesive and self-directed teams

- Communication skills (includes effective listening)

- Sales training basics (everybody sells)

RETENTION THROUGH TRAINING
(continued)

These four programs are not that difficult to implement. If your company does not have the resources to develop these programs, outside consultants can provide training in these areas. To find these consultants, contact your local chapter of the American Society for Training and Development (ASTD) or your local colleges and junior colleges. One of these organizations will be able to direct you to qualified trainers who can help you develop and implement employee training programs in conjunction with your customer service and retention program.

If you decide to work with an outside consultant or trainer to upgrade the skills of your employees, you will probably go through the same process that others go through when they decide to do business with you. People choose to do business with someone for reasons such as convenience, price, location, or personal referral. Remember that when people choose you, they are your customers, and when you choose a trainer for your company, you are that trainer's customer.

The evaluation criteria questionnaire that follows represents the processes people go through when selecting a consultant or a business provider. Answer these questions accurately. They will help you select the person or training firm you need.

EVALUATION CRITERIA QUESTIONNAIRE

1. Does the consultant (business) demonstrate complete understanding of my problem, situation or needs?

2. Has the consultant (business) fully and accurately explained the approach (product or service) that will solve my problem?

3. Do I think the proposed approach will be successful?

4. What resources are available to make me a satisfied customer?

5. Is the consultant (business) qualified to provide me with the products and services I need?

6. Is the behavioral, communication and service style of the consultant (business) compatible with my own?

7. Will my problem be solved, or will my needs be met quickly?

8. Is the consultant (business) experienced enough for my situation?

9. Is the cost of the product or service fair, and am I getting good value for my money?

10. Do the references of the consultant (business) confirm the level and quality of service that I will be receiving?

Use these questions as a guide when selecting a trainer to develop the skills of your employees. Choose your consultant carefully. Remember—when you train your employees, they will perceive that you truly care about them. Not only will they provide superior service to your customers, they will also provide you with superior performance, productivity and loyalty. When you train your staff well, you, your business, your employees, your customers—everyone—wins.

RAPPORT AND EFFECTIVE COMMUNICATION

Every time you interact with a customer it is a moment of truth. It is a chance for you or your employees to represent the company positively and to satisfy a customer. These interactions will succeed or fail depending on how well rapport is established and how effectively you communicate with the customer. The skills for building rapport and strengthening communication are easily learned.

When a customer comes to you to make or exchange a purchase, request information or register a complaint, that customer wants to be heard. You must be an active and attentive listener so you can understand how the customer perceives the current situation, even though you may perceive it differently.

You and your customer each interpret any given situation based on your behavioral style and sensory perceptual style. We are all a combination of four behavioral styles: Relational, Expressive, Analytical or Dominant. Certain characteristics make up each type, which are shown in the Personality Factors chart on the next page. You can remember the names of each type with the acronym R.E.A.D.

You must know how to respond to your customers based on their particular behavioral styles. For example, a dominant customer is impatient and wants to control the situation to ensure he or she gets the desired results. Analytical types will be very precise and compliant with your rules for customer service and can be extremely persistent with their questioning. The Service Situation Planner on page 68 will help you respond to each behavioral type.

If you can respond appropriately to each behavioral type, you will develop rapport with that person. You can increase this rapport by "pacing" your customer. Pacing means that you mirror their body language, rate of speech, vocal tones and even eye movements.

Try to use the same words, phrases, slogans and slang your customers use, because their words will tell you their sensory perceptual style: visual, auditory or kinesthetic. A visual person speaks in pictures, images and sights. An auditory person talks about sounds, hearing and harmony. A kinesthetic person describes a situation in terms of feelings, senses and touch.

Behavioral Styles: Personality Factors

DOMINANT

- Goal oriented/results oriented
- Impatient
- Task oriented/high achiever
- Workaholic
- Decisive
- Opinionated/stubborn/blunt
- Innovative
- Tough/firm in relationships
- Control oriented
- Competitive/loves challenges

EXPRESSIVE

- Dreamer; unrealistic goals
- Craves Recognition
- Creative; ideas flow
- Needs approval and compliments
- Generalizes
- Persuasive, outgoing
- Opinionated
- Fast decisions
- Excitable
- Enthusiastic, shows confidence

RELATIONAL

- Needs people
- Good listener
- Status quo/dislikes change
- No risks
- No pressure
- Counselor/helps others
- Questioning
- Insecure/needs reassurance
- Supportive
- No conflict

ANALYTICAL

- Planner/organizer/sequencer
- Details/technicalities
- Slow decisions
- Must be right
- Conservative/cautious
- Low pressure
- Precise/critical/logical
- Problem solver
- Persistent
- Follows procedures/compliant

Behavioral Styles: Service Situation Planner

"D" DOMINANT	"E" EXPRESSIVE
Be clear, specific, brief and efficient.	Plan interaction that supports their feelings/intuitions. Be stimulating. Use enough time to be sociable, yet fast-moving.
Stick to business.	
Present the facts logically.	Leave time for relating, socializing after completing service encounter.
Ask specific (preferably "what") questions. Provide service choices.	Talk about people, their goals, opinions they find stimulating.
Provide facts and figures about the results of your service.	Don't discuss extensive details related to service. Ask for their opinions/ideas regarding how to service them better.
If you disagree, take issue with facts, not the person.	Provide ideas for implementing action.
Motivate and persuade by referring to objectives and results.	Provide testimonials from people they perceive as important, prominent.
Support, maintain, use discretion.	Offer special, immediate and extra incentives for their willingness to accept your service offer.
	Continue supporting the relationship, be casual.
	Recognize their accomplishments.

"R" RELATIONAL	"A" ANALYTICAL
Start (briefly) with a personal commitment. Be agreeable.	Approach them in a straightforward, direct but low keyed way; stick to business.
Show sincere interest in them as people.	Support their logical, methodical approach; build your credibility by listing pros and cons of your service approach.
Listen well. Be responsive and supportive.	
Elicit personal goals and work to help achieve these goals as related to service.	Present specifics and do what you say you can do. Take your time, but be persistent.
Ask "how" questions.	Create a schedule to implement service actions with step-by-step timetable. Assure them there won't be surprises.
If you agree easily, look for possible areas of their disagreement or dissatisfaction.	
If you disagree, look for hurt feelings.	If you agree, follow through and document for the record.
Be informal, orderly and friendly.	If you disagree, make an organized presentation of your position and ask for their suggestions to resolve the situation.
Guarantee their decision will minimize risks.	
Offer clear, specific solutions with guarantees.	Give them time to verify predictability of your actions; be accurate, realistic.
	Provide solid, tangible, practical evidence and options for future service performance.
	Provide long-term guarantees.

Rapport and effective communication is enhanced when you use the same types of words your customer uses. If your customer says, "It sounds to me like this product is not working properly," do not respond, "I see what you are saying." You answer, "I hear what you are saying. What sound tells you the product is not working properly?"

When you establish good rapport and communication with your customers, they will want to continue doing business with you and will refer others to you. The result is more business and more customers staying with you for a longer period of time.

When your customers say they enjoy doing business with you because you are so much like them, you understand them, you know almost exactly what they are thinking and you provide excellent service, you have received one of the greatest compliments any businessperson can receive from a customer.

Remember, more often than not, people do business with people they like and who are most like them.

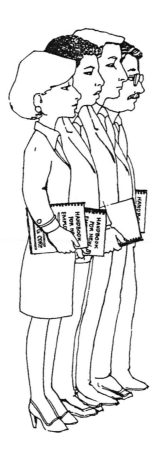

SENSORY PERCEPTUAL STYLE PROCESSOR EQUIVALENTS

Every sensory perceptual style has its own language by which it processes information. The language of one style has an equivalent in the other two styles. These are called processor equivalents. It is up to you, and necessary for your complete understanding of sensory perceptual styles, to identify these and other terms related to each particular style. For example, anything having to do with seeing or images is visual, hearing or sounds or speaking is auditory, and feeling or touch is kinesthetic. The list below provides you with some of these processor equivalents. Once you identify that the words someone uses belong to a specific sensory perceptual style, you must match those words and style to achieve rapport. This mean you may have to change your sensory perceptual communication style for a particular situation, because you want to communicate successfully.

VISUAL	AUDITORY	KINESTHETIC
See	Hear	Feel
Look	Listen	Touch
Bright	Loud	Pressing
Picture	Sound	Feeling
Colorful	Melodious	Exciting
Illuminate	Be heard	Be felt
Clear	Harmonious	Fits
Dawn	Tune in	Firm
Flash	Crescendo	Spike
Appear	Discuss	Aware
Perspective	Expression	Hands-on
Focused	Listen to	Secure
Foggy	Off-key	Clumsy
Strobe	Harsh	Irritate
Form	Resonance	Angle
Visual	Vocal	Do/act
Imagine	Speak	Be
Perception	Attention	Action
Blank out	Inner voices	Fidget

TIPS FOR LONG-TERM CUSTOMER RETENTION

► Call each customer by name.

► Listen to what each customer has to say.

► Be concerned about each customer as an individual.

► Be courteous to each customer.

► Be responsive to the individual needs of each customer.

► Know your customers' personal buying histories and motivations.

► Take sufficient time with each customer.

► Involve customers in your business. Ask for their advice and suggestions.

► Make customers feel important. Pay them compliments.

► Listen first to understand the customer. Then speak so they can understand you.

10 COMMANDMENTS OF SUPERIOR CUSTOMER SERVICE AND RETENTION

1. The customer is the most important person in the company.

2. The customer is not dependent on you—you are dependent on the customer. You work for the customer.

3. The customer is not an interruption of your work. The customer is the purpose of your work.

4. The customer does you a favor by visiting or calling your business. You are not doing the customer a favor by serving them.

5. The customer is as much a part of your business as anything else, including inventory, employees and your facility. If you sold the business, the customers would go with it.

6. The customer is not a cold statistic. The customer is a person with feelings and emotions, just like you. Treat the customer better than you would want to be treated.

7. The customer is not someone to argue with or match wits with.

8. It is your job to satisfy the needs, wants and expectations of your customers and, whenever possible, resolve their fears and complaints.

9. The customer deserves the most attentive, courteous and professional treatment you can provide.

10. The customer is the lifeblood of your business. Always remember that without customers, you would not have a business. You work for the customer.

IV

50 Ways to
Keep Your Customers

YOUR KEY TO LONG-LASTING SUCCESS

It has been said many times throughout the book, but it is worth repeating again: your only purpose for being in business is to get and keep customers. Without customers, you have no business. So, you must focus everything you do toward finding out exactly what your customers need, want and expect from you, and then you must give them all that and more.

Once you've acquired them as customers, you must do everything possible to keep them for life. We've already talked about ways to create customer commitment and sustain customer loyalty. Reward and recognition programs, thank you notes, newsletters, customer councils, and other programs and techniques will all work in your favor.

Yet, sometimes it seems that whatever you do, it's never quite enough.

There's always someone, somewhere, who comes up with a new and better way to serve customers. Then, your customers start asking you when they'll receive those products, programs or services, or at least something comparable. You, of course, want to do everything you can to give them what they want, but it may not be possible within your current system.

I strongly recommend that you find a way to serve that customer or those customers. It may take some planning and creativity, but when you do, you'll get a customer for life.

Customer Retention Strategies and Tactics

In a moment, you'll read a list of 50 ways you can keep customers for life. Do what you must to make them work for your business. Adapt them as you need to. Just make sure you implement as many of these recommendations as possible on a daily basis. When you do, you'll not only retain customers for life, you'll turn them into recommenders and advocates.

CUSTOMER ADVOCATES AND RECOMMENDERS

Because you have already learned many ways to keep customers for life and to outservice your competition, I want you to strive for an even higher goal where your customers are concerned. Your goal is to now take your satisfied, loyal and committed customers and turn them into advocates and recommenders.

Advocates are customers who go out and talk about your business on their own. They don't necessarily refer people to you. They're just out there telling the world about how great you treat them, how wonderful it is to do business with you, and how you're the best thing in the world.

When you find these customers, you may want to give them their own business cards that say Customer Advocate. You might give them a stack of discount coupons to give out as they see fit. These people then become your best unpaid sales force, and they are much more credible than your in-house sales team because they have nothing to gain from advocating and recommending your business. Of course, you'll want to find some way to recognize and reward their efforts.

You need advocates. They are your counterbalance to any customer who is dissatisfied with your service and wants to tell 10–20 other people about their negative experience with you. The advocates can tell those same people how wonderful you really are and possibly overcome the negative influence.

Recommenders are slightly different from advocates. These are people who agree to allow potential customers to call them for a "credibility check" on you and your business. Let's say you have a prospect who can become a customer, but who wants to talk with some of your other customers first. Standard procedure is to give the prospect a list of references who will say nice, positive things about you. Develop a list of recommenders who will allow a prospect to call them at work or at home. Then, when they receive the call, they promote your business and say wonderful things about you and your staff.

These recommenders should be long-term and loyal customers, but they don't always have to be. A recommender can be anyone who is extremely satisfied with what you've done and is willing to be available to tell anyone else who calls. The longer they've been with you, the more they know about your business and how you run it. This gives them insights which they can pass on to the prospect in a way your sales staff can't. Plus, the positive comments about the business coming from other customers makes everything all the more credible.

50 WAYS TO KEEP YOUR CUSTOMERS FOR LIFE

You're almost there. So far, we've talked about customer service and going beyond customer service. Now here's a list of 50 things you can do to secure, satisfy, and retain your customers for life.

1. CREATE A SERVICE-ORIENTED CULTURE.

Everyone in the company must be customer-service oriented. All employees must realize that they work for the customer, and their job is to ensure the ultimate satisfaction of the customer. Everything else is superfluous.

2. HAVE A SERVICE VISION.

A vision is vital to the service success of any organization. A vision is more than just a philosophy of doing business. The vision must be the corporate cultural ethic. Everyone must believe and live the vision for your company to provide excellent customer service and keep customers for life. Management may develop the vision, but the staff must make it a reality.

3. POLICIES IN WRITING.

To benefit both your customers and your employees, put your service policies in writing. This way, there can be no mistakes or misunderstandings. Be aware, however, that your employees should have the authority to grant discretionary exceptions to the policies when the need arises. Remember, policies are guidelines, and they must remain flexible.

4. EMPLOYEE EMPOWERMENT.

Give your employees the authority to go with their responsibility of satisfying and keeping the customer. Allow them to make decisions on the spot and support those decisions. Remember, their job is to satisfy the customers and keep them coming back. Employees should not have to look for you or a manager every time a customer needs something out of the ordinary.

50 WAYS TO KEEP YOUR CUSTOMERS FOR LIFE (continued)

5. EMPLOYEE TRAINING.

Train, train and then retrain to retain your employees. Give them on-the-job training, off-the-job training, tapes, books, seminars, workshops, anything that will help them do their jobs better. While you may find qualified people who have just graduated from school, nothing prepares a person better for handling customers than the training they receive on the job and in practically applied programs.

6. MARKETING THE SERVICE PROGRAM.

All of your marketing should communicate that you provide superior customer service, are interested only in total customer satisfaction, and will do everything possible to keep your customers. This message must be stated in everything you send out to the public and the trades.

7. HIRE GOOD PEOPLE.

Hire people who are good and well qualified. Innate people skills go a long way toward helping your staff provide superior customer service and retain your customers.

8. DON'T MAKE CUSTOMERS PAY FOR SERVICE.

Pay for anything related to customer service, including shipping charges on returns, long-distance telephone calls, postage, and anything else for which the customer is normally charged. If you don't pay for the cost of service, your competition will, and then your customers will become their customers.

9. REWARD LOYALTY.

What gets rewarded gets done. If you reward both customers and employees for their loyalty, they will stay with you a long time. The rewards must be perceived as valuable by the recipient, but they do not have to cost you much money.

10. SET STANDARDS OF PERFORMANCE.

Let everyone know exactly what they must do to provide superior customer service. Make these standards as objective and measurable as possible, even though you may provide an intangible service. When people achieve these performance levels, customer retention and loyalty naturally follow.

11. TRADE JOBS.

Have your employees work in other departments. They will develop an appreciation for what other people in the company do, and therefore no employee will blame another for a customer problem. In fact, since the employees have experience in other areas, they will be able to solve more problems and satisfy more customers on the spot.

12. USER FRIENDLY SERVICE SYSTEMS.

Make your customer service systems easy to use. The customer is the reason for your business, not someone who is in the way of doing business. Make the customers feel and know they can bring a problem to your attention, voice a complaint, get it resolved as quickly as possible and receive superb treatment during all their contacts with your company.

13. DESIGN FLEXIBILITY INTO YOUR SERVICE POLICIES.

Keep your policies flexible, because each customer and situation is different. Your employees must know they can modify a written or stated policy to ensure the customer's total satisfaction at any given moment, and you must support your employees' decisions and actions in these situations.

14. EDUCATE THE CUSTOMER.

Do not assume the customer knows what you know. Use every customer contact as a chance to educate the customer about something related to your business. Even if you are just educating them about your great return policy, teach them. They will be appreciative and show this by continuing to do business with you.

50 WAYS TO KEEP YOUR CUSTOMERS FOR LIFE (continued)

15. HANDLE COMPLAINTS PROPERLY.

Acknowledge that the customer is upset, listen carefully, assure them you are doing everything possible at this moment to resolve their complaint, and then resolve the complaint. Then, when they express appreciation for your efforts, use the opportunity to increase their loyalty. Thank them for bringing the problem to your attention, apologize again for the problem, and try to sell them something else.

16. TURN COMPLAINTS INTO ADDITIONAL SALES.

The customer is most receptive to continuing to do business with you after you resolve a complaint. Using this opportunity to make a sale is both ethical and practical. Your customers will appreciate your interest in them. They will probably buy from you now and go out and tell their friends how well and quickly you handled their problem. You will develop a reputation with customers of credibility, reliability and honesty.

17. TRAIN YOUR EMPLOYEES TO DO IT RIGHT THE FIRST TIME.

Repair, rework and additional free services are very costly. Doing it right the first time guarantees greater profitability, happier customers and more long-term customers. If you must do something over again for a customer, do it even "righter" the second time.

18. BEG FOR CUSTOMER FEEDBACK.

It is not enough to send out surveys or leave comment cards at the cash register. You must get as much customer feedback as possible, even if you have to beg for it. If customers are asked their opinion and see that you have implemented their suggestions, they will not only continue to do business with you, they will recommend that friends come to you also. Do whatever you can to solicit their opinions and comments, and then act on their suggestions.

19. GET AND USE EMPLOYEE IDEAS.

Your employees who have daily contact with customers know more about what customers need, want and expect than you or any other manager could ever hope to know. Get feedback from your employees, listen carefully to their suggestions, and implement as many as possible. Research shows that the best service companies not only get more ideas from their employees, they use more of them. This makes employees feel wanted and cared about and shows them that you think as much of your internal customers as you do your external customers.

20. BE FAIR AND CONSISTENT.

Customers may not always like or agree with what you do for them, but as long as you treat each one fairly and consistently, they will respect you for it. Consistency enhances your credibility and reliability which are essential for building loyalty and retaining customers.

21. UNDERPROMISE AND OVERDELIVER.

Customers' expectations can be unrealistically raised when businesses overpromise and underdeliver. Usually, the business cannot meet these expectations, and the customer goes away disappointed. But if you set realistic expectations for the customer on your quality and level of service and then exceed those expectations, the customer is more than satisfied. Remember, though, that you should not underpromise to the extent that you insult your customers. They will see through you in a minute and take their business elsewhere.

22. COMPETE ON BENEFITS, NOT PRODUCTS OR PRICES.

Customers can always find another product at a lower price, somehow, somewhere. You must always remind your customers of the benefits of doing business with you. Features can be found in every product, but benefits are unique to the way you do business.

50 WAYS TO KEEP YOUR CUSTOMERS FOR LIFE (continued)

23. HIGH TOUCH IS MORE IMPORTANT THAN HIGH TECH.

High tech does get people to say "WOW!", but it doesn't get people to care about other people. Your business needs high touch to survive. Stay close to your customers. Get to know them well. The closer you are to your customers, the longer they will do business with you. After all, when you show you care, you become like one of the family.

24. KNOW THE COST OF LOSING A CUSTOMER.

All employees should know the lifetime value of a customer, the cost of losing even one, and the effect that loss can have on your business. Consider rewarding your employees if they retain your customers over a longer-than-average time period.

25. KNOW YOUR COMPETITION.

What kinds of customer services are your competitors providing? What are they doing to retain their customers? Are they offering more benefits, better service policies, or are they just being nicer to the customers? Find out, and if they are doing something you are not doing, then do it. If it works for them, it will probably work for you.

26. CONDUCT INTERNAL ASSESSMENTS.

Constantly evaluate your company's customer service, satisfaction and retention. Interview your employees, have them fill out questionnaires, ask your customers at the point of purchase how you are doing, and then use this information to improve your service and retention efforts. Examples of simple surveys for you to use are provided in Appendix A.

27. KNOW WHAT YOUR CUSTOMERS NEED, WANT, AND EXPECT.

Businesses run into problems when they think customers need, want or expect one thing, yet they really require another. These gaps in perceptions about service delivery ultimately disappoint customers. Find out what the customers need, want and expect, and then give it to them.

28. FIND, NURTURE AND DISPLAY CUSTOMER CHAMPIONS.

Every business has one, two or several employees who are true customer champions. Find out who these people are, nurture and support them, then make them role models for everyone else to follow. Reward their behavior. The rest of your staff will upgrade their service performance to this level to receive similar rewards. The result is a highly motivated, service-oriented staff and a group of satisfied and loyal customers.

29. EFFECTIVE COMMUNICATION IS CRITICAL TO SUCCESS.

Every problem between people is the result of poor communication. Train your people to develop effective communication skills: how to listen first, how to speak so others will listen, how to understand others before trying to be understood, how to receive and give feedback, and how to develop rapport with customers.

30. SMILE.

Smiling is important when serving a customer. Smiles will usually get a smile in return, but smiles will not guarantee quality customer service. Smiling must be something employees do because it makes them feel good, and it makes the customers feel good.

31. MAKE CUSTOMERS FEEL IMPORTANT.

The more important you make customers feel, the better they will feel about doing business with you. Call them by name, ask them to tell you about themselves and ask questions about their accomplishments. Your reward will be a lifetime customer.

32. PROMOTE YOUR CUSTOMERS.

With their permission, of course, use your customers in your marketing and promotion efforts. Let them tell their story to other customers and prospects. This third party endorsement fosters tremendous credibility, and your customers will love being involved.

50 WAYS TO KEEP YOUR CUSTOMERS FOR LIFE (continued)

33. CREATE A CUSTOMER COUNCIL.

Your customer council, which is like a board of directors or focus group, should meet regularly to scrutinize your business and the service you provide. The council makes suggestions on which you act.

34. MARKET FREQUENT BUYER PROGRAMS.

To get your customers excited about doing business with you, start a reward program for frequent buyers. You can use coupons, punch cards or anything else that helps you keep track of customer activity. When purchases reach a certain level, reward your customers with a gift—a deep discount coupon, a free product or service or something more expensive, such as a trip.

35. ACCEPT ONLY EXCELLENCE.

If you expect average performance and service, that is what you will get. Therefore, set your expectations high. Accept only excellent performance from your employees, and train your staff to achieve these levels of performance. Good enough should never be good enough.

36. EMPLOYEES ARE CUSTOMERS, TOO.

Employees are your internal customers, your first line of customers, and each of them has a customer somewhere in the value chain. Each employee must provide excellent customer service to every other employee so that they all can provide superior service to customers. This is the only way to guarantee customer satisfaction and retention.

37. LET CUSTOMERS KNOW YOU CARE.

Send them thank you cards, holiday cards and anything else you can to show them you care. Never let them forget your name. Teach them that whenever they need something, they can come to you for it because you care. Spend time and money marketing your caring attitude to your customers.

38. MAKE SERVICE RESULTS VISIBLE.

Visibility enhances credibility, and credibility is only enhanced by improved performance. Post your customer comment cards and letters for all customers to see. Create a testimonial book for customers to read. Post employees' performance results in their lounge or locker room. Make service results visible so that your employees will constantly improve and your customers will be the beneficiaries of this improved service.

39. GO THE EXTRA MILE.

When customers want something from you, give it to them. Then do something extra. They will be grateful and you will have a long term customer.

40. MARKETING AND CUSTOMER SERVICE GO HAND IN HAND.

All of your marketing efforts should communicate your customer service message. In today's competitive marketplace, the only thing that differentiates companies is the level and quality of their customer service, and this is the major criteria people use to decide whether or not to continue purchasing from that company. Customer service is a very effective and powerful marketing tool, and marketing is a very effective and powerful customer service tool. Combined, the two will help you keep your customers for life.

41. SELECT THE RIGHT CUSTOMERS

Some customers are simply more profitable for you to do business with, while others just drain your energy and your profits. Try to identify those customers who will spend more, complain less, refer more, and stay with you longer. Then, do whatever you must to serve and satisfy them so they become loyal, lifetime customers.

50 WAYS TO KEEP YOUR CUSTOMERS FOR LIFE (continued)

42. MOVE CUSTOMERS FROM SATISFACTION TO LOYALTY.

Having satisfied customers is not always enough. You must move them from being satisfied to being loyal. Loyalty means they spend more money with you more often than they do with your competitors. Loyalty means you've developed a high level of trust with your customers. And, loyalty means you and your customers work together as "strategic partners."

43. MEASURE WHAT IS IMPORTANT TO THE CUSTOMER.

Most businesses take measurements on their own performances so they can "improve." However, the measures a business focuses on may not be what's important to their customers. Ask your customers what you should be measuring, then measure that, then make improvements that the customers can see.

44. KNOW WHAT CUSTOMERS REALLY WANT IN THEIR RELATIONSHIP WITH YOU.

Customers want certain things when they buy a product, and other things when they purchase a service. If you sell a product, provide high value, superior quality, and reliability. If you sell a service, provide a guarantee, have a mechanism for resolving complaints readily available, and establish high levels of trust.

45. KNOW YOUR CUSTOMER DEFECTION REASONS AND PATTERNS.

While many businesses are simply calculating attrition or customer turnover, you can keep more of your customers when you identify the reasons for their defections as well as the rates. Determine why customers are leaving you, when they are leaving, and where they are going. Then, create the programs and services that will reduce these defection rates and interrupt these defection patterns.

46. CONDUCT A FAILURE ANALYSIS ON YOUR BUSINESS.

The truth is we learn more from our mistakes than our successes. Failure analysis determines where and why we made certain mistakes, and what we should do about them. Remember, nothing is ever true failure unless we neglect to learn from it. Get everyone involved in the analysis and subsequent learning.

47. KNOW YOUR RETENTION IMPROVEMENT MEASURES.

After you calculate defection rates and patterns, you need to know what to measure for retention improvement. In addition to retention rates, you need to know your customer tenure rate (how long they stay with you) and the customer class half life (how long it takes half of the customers you gain in a given time period to defect to your competitors). When you have all this information, you can develop effective retention improvement programs.

48. DEVELOP A MARKET VALUE PRICING MODEL FOR YOUR BUSINESS.

You know that not all customers are created equal. And, not all customers should pay the same thing for your products or services. In fact, if you carefully segment your customers, you will find that some are willing to pay more for the same products and services. When you establish this variable pricing model based on value to the customer, your profitability will increase and so will the loyalty of your customers. That's because they perceive that you're giving them extra service and value, plus pricing your items especially for them.

49. KNOW YOUR PURPOSE FOR BEING IN BUSINESS.

It may sound like a cliché, but the best way you can get and keep customers for life is to know and realize that your one purpose for being in business is to get, satisfy and keep loyal customers. Do whatever it takes to achieve this goal. Keep your eyes on the customers, not the money, and the money will always be there.

50. DO WHAT WORKS ALL OVER AGAIN.

Don't reinvent the wheel. Figure out which of these 50 activities is working best for you and continue to do it or them repeatedly. Simple is best. Are there some more you can think of?

A FINAL THOUGHT ABOUT RETENTION

There's no question in anyone's mind that the customer is the focal point of your business. Without customers, you have no business. So it just makes sense to do everything you can to keep them loyal and committed to you for life, or at least as long as possible.

This book has provided you with hundreds of ways to create superior customer service programs, to use customer service as a powerful marketing tool, and to position your business as a high quality service provider so customers will choose you over the competition. Now it is up to you to put all these ideas into practice to keep your customers for life.

Begin your journey to long-term customer retention by developing retention programs for your business. Make sure your efforts are active rather than reactive, as I describe in the next section. Then, before you read about 10 things you should do to create customer service and retention management programs, fill in the chart about what your business is doing now. This exercise will help you to develop the programs you need. Then examine the lists and see how you can adapt them to make them more useful to your business.

Constant Improvement

Customer service can always be improved, which will lead to ever-increasing levels of customer satisfaction. Never think that you can sit back just because your latest survey told you your customers were satisfied. If you know they're satisfied, you've got to go out and find out how to make them more satisfied—and even if they're satisfied, they may not be totally loyal.

We know that customers will appreciate your efforts and your thank-yous (cards, gifts, other rewards). There's something else you must do to make sure customers stay with you and remain loyal. You must increase the perceived value of their psychological switching costs.

A customer will buy your product or service from a competitor to save even a small amount of money, but if the customer is psychologically "attached" to your business, then the psychological cost associated with switching to your competitor become too great. Interviews conducted with customers reveal these themes:

"They treat me like family."

"They know my name."

"They sent me a birthday card."

"They really do appreciate my business."

"They always pay attention to me when I come in. The staff never gets impatient, even when I don't know exactly what I want."

You get the idea. There's a strong psychological component to customer service and long-term customer retention. Each of the above comments relates to fulfilling a psychological need, such as feeling important or appreciated, of being recognized, and of being included. If you looked at your own business and its customers, you can probably identify other psychological needs that you can fill.

Customers are the lifeblood of your business. Service is the vehicle that keeps the blood pumping. Superior customer service, proactive retention programs, using service as a marketing tool, and going out of your way to get, satisfy and keep your customers will make your business successful for years to come.

10 More Ways to Provide Great Customer Service

1. Inspect what you expect.

2. Educate the customer about your great customer service and how to use it.

3. Identify customer values, beliefs, and standards and match them to your own.

4. Manage service daily and track results.

5. Conduct customer and market research to find out what's going on out there.

6. Promote your customers to others.

7. Give better-than-risk-free guarantees.

8. Anticipate changes in customer needs and be ready to serve them.

9. Visit customers on their "turf."

10. Keep in touch with customers.

25 CUSTOMER RETENTION PROGRAMS THAT WORK

Now that you've read about the importance of providing great customer service, how it affects your business and bottom line, and what you must do to make certain your staff takes care of your customers, it's time to describe retention programs that work to lower your attrition rate. Implementing any of these programs will help you retain your customers. Combining several of these programs or running them in succession will also help you keep your customers for life.

Here are 25 ways you can program customer retention into your business operations.

1. **SPECIAL EVENTS**—Create special events just to show customers how special they are to you. There is no one type of event that will be more successful than another. You need to use your creativity and ingenuity to develop these events and make them work.

2. **VALUE-ADDED SERVICES**—Customers must perceive that they receive more for their money than they expected. Some value-added services include free valet parking, free coffee, free local phone calls, free car wash, closed captioning on your television sets, parent/child events, educational classes, and unique training seminars. What you do depends on the type of business you run.

3. **BUDDY SYSTEM/MENTORS**—New customers often defect because the do not feel comfortable in your place of business. Assign a customer advocate to be a buddy or mentor to the new customer for the first month or two. You can also use a staff person in the mentor role. The new customer will love the personal attention and stay with you longer.

4. **NEW CUSTOMER ORIENTATION PLAN**—Many businesses have a staff person teach new customers how to use their purchase. Develop a longer term orientation program that keeps the new customer learning over a period of weeks instead of minutes. As long as the new customer is gaining knowledge, they'll stay motivated. This will translate into greater satisfaction and greater retention. For example, automobile dealerships can conduct workshops for new owners in how to get the greatest benefit from the service department.

25 CUSTOMER RETENTION PROGRAMS THAT WORK (continued)

5. **EDUCATION CLASSES**—Hold classes on topics of interest to your customers: financial, business operations, marketing, relationships, selling, raising children, and anything else you can think of.

6. **COMPUTERIZED TRACKING**—No matter how proficient people become on computers, they still love to get their own printouts on their achievements. Plus, a computerized tracking system lets customers know you're interested in the technology that will help them achieve their goals. So, give them a printout of their purchase history. You will be pleasantly surprised at their reaction.

7. **THE NAME GAME**—Require your staff to learn the names of at least 5 new customers each day. When your staff can call every customer by their name, then the customers will continue to stay with your because of the personal recognition they receive.

8. **TOUCH ME IN THE MORNING**—Make sure your staff "touches" at least 5 new customers a day. They can physically touch them, on the elbow or shoulder during a visit, or they can emotionally touch them. All customers want respect and recognition.

9. **TRUST**—Establish programs and policies that show your customers you trust them. This could relate to payments, use of equipment, or anything else. The more trust you show toward customers, the more they'll stay with you. Would you want to go somewhere else where you have to prove yourself to new owners and staff when your current business trusts you implicitly?

10. **GREAT CUSTOMER SERVICE**—Do whatever it takes to serve and satisfy customers, and you'll be rewarded with their loyalty, commitment and long-term purchases.

11. **MAKE SHOPPING WITH YOU FUN**—Make your business a fun place to be. If you can take the drudgery out of doing business with you, you can put more customers in your business for longer periods of time.

12. INSTRUCTION—Have your staff make personal contact with each customer in the business and offer encouragement plus a bit of advice on how to improve their shopping experience. Customers will appreciate the personal touch and stay with you to continue to receive it.

13. CONTESTS—Develop contests for your customers. Change the contest environment so one person doesn't always win. When more people can win a contest, more people will stay involved. Award prizes that have a high perceived value without being expensive.

14. MEDIA COVERAGE—Some of your customers won't mind having their names in the paper or being on radio or TV. Find out who these people are and make them stars of your business. They'll reward you with loyalty and long-term purchases. When their friends see them on TV or read about them in the paper, they'll probably buy from you just for the chance to be a star.

15. EMPOWERED EMPLOYEES—Train your employees well, then empower them to make decisions to serve the customers. Next, provide your employees with the authority to support their responsibility of serving and satisfying the customers. When employees are truly empowered, they feel better about themselves, which translates into better customer service.

16. CUSTOMER FEEDBACK—Involve your customers in the business. Get them on an advisory council, solicit their feedback for business improvements, and implement their suggestions. By involving them, you provide them with an "ownership" stake, and they will stay with you longer because now they have a part in helping you succeed.

17. AT-HOME SERVICES—Instead of letting customers go elsewhere, for whatever reason, offer them an "at-home shopping" experience. This can range from sending a personal shopper to their home on a scheduled basis to providing home delivery.

25 CUSTOMER RETENTION PROGRAMS THAT WORK (continued)

18. **CANCELLATION FEES**—Let customers know that you're so interested in keeping them for the long term that you will charge them a fee to stop doing business with you. This will help·them think twice about leaving you and giving up their customer benefits. It also works best with subscription or membership type businesses.

19. **ZERO ATTRITION**—While your business industry attrition rates vary, you can set a goal of 0% attrition. Is this impossible to reach? I don't know. What I do know is that if you set a goal for 25% attrition and you achieve it, you'll get complacent. The only way to achieve zero attrition is to set it as a goal and strive for it.

20. **RECALL AND CONFIRMATION CALLS**—If your customer database suggests that certain customers have not been in for a while, call them, write them, or even go visit them to learn why not. Schedule appointments for them to come in and see you personally. Offer them something for free as an inducement to come back to the business. Always remember to use your computer as a tracking, marketing and retention tool. Businesses constantly leave tons of money on the table (or in the computer) by not accessing this information.

21. **BUSINESSES OR CLUBS WITHIN THE BUSINESS**—Form special interest groups or clubs. Establish cycling clubs, hiking clubs, investment clubs, or any other type of club you can think of to get customers involved with each other. The more things you can provide for the customers, and the more reasons they have to come to your business, the longer they'll stay with you.

22. **SUMMER CAMP**—If you can find a way to hold a summer camp for adults and children, do it. Parents everywhere look for places to send their children when school is out. What better place than a special type of camp run or sponsored by your business, where they already trust the staff. Aside from keeping customers with you longer, summer camp can be a nice revenue generator for the business.

23. COMMUNITY OUTREACH PROGRAMS—Use this marketing tool more effectively by promoting your community services to your customers. People like to do business with companies that give something back to the community. Your outreach programs can be as simple as sponsoring a youth sports team or as complex as hosting a health or business fair. Whatever you do, your in-house promotions of your work will motivate customers to stay with you.

24. NAMES IN THE NEWS—Most businesses have a newsletter or bulletin board. If you don't, get one. Put new customers' names in the newsletter, as well as the names of those who refer other customers to you. People love to see their name in print, and they'll continue to try to gain that recognition again. When you do put customers' names in the newsletter, send them a paste-up of the page with the masthead. They'll appreciate your extra effort.

25. RETRAIN TO RETAIN—After training staff to perform their duties, retrain them to work as if they were 5-star hotel personnel. To do this quickly and inexpensively, send your staff to any of these hotels, have them sit in the lobby, eat in the restaurants, and observe the quality of the service. When they bring these techniques back to your business, you'll see a vast improvement in their skills as well as their morale. Provide this retraining and you'll also see your customer satisfaction ratings soar and your customer retention levels rise.

Are there some more you can think of?

A P P E N D I X

A

Customer Service, Satisfaction and Retention Inventories

The importance of self-assessment and evaluation cannot be overemphasized. The following series of surveys will help you evaluate your customer service efforts, including how well you provide service, how well your staff provides service, and how satisfied your customers are with your service. The results of these surveys will indicate your customer service strengths and weaknesses. In all surveys, the higher the number the more favorable the response. Feel free to adapt the surveys to suit your particular needs.

CUSTOMER SERVICE SELF-ASSESSMENT

Respond to each statement by placing the number that best describes your answer in the space provided. Use the following scale:

1	2	3	4	5
Never	Rarely	Sometimes	Usually	Often

_____ 1. I accept people without judging them.

_____ 2. I show patience, courtesy and respect to people regardless of their behavior toward me.

_____ 3. I maintain my composure and refuse to become irritated or frustrated when coping with an angry or irate person.

_____ 4. I treat people as I would want them to treat me.

_____ 5. I help others maintain their self-esteem, even when the situation requires negative or critical feedback.

_____ 6. I do not get defensive when interacting with another person, even if their comments are directed at me.

_____ 7. I realize that my attitude toward myself and others affects the way I respond in any given situation.

_____ 8. I realize that each person believes his or her problem is the most important and urgent thing in the world at this time, and I attempt to help them resolve it immediately.

_____ 9. I treat everyone in a positive manner, regardless of how they look, dress or speak.

_____ 10. I view every interaction with another person as a "golden moment," and I do everything in my power to make it a satisfactory and win-win situation for both of us.

SERVICE RATING SCALE

Using a scale of 1 to 10 with 10 being the best, please rate how well you and your staff provide each of the following services:

Service	Self	Staff
a. Prompt and courteous answering of the telephones	_____	_____
b. Accurate responses to telephone inquiries	_____	_____
c. Providing individualized and personalized attention to each client	_____	_____
d. Marketing and promoting the business to current and new clients	_____	_____
e. Marketing and promoting the business to professional and other referral sources	_____	_____
f. Communicating prices and billing procedures clearly and concisely	_____	_____
g. Providing high quality, courteous and friendly service to all clients	_____	_____
h. Requesting and quickly resolving customer complaints	_____	_____
i. Keeping clients informed and updated about current and new developments regarding the business	_____	_____
j. Tracking the effectiveness of marketing and service efforts	_____	_____

CUSTOMER SERVICE INVENTORY

We are interested in finding out what you think about our services. Please respond to each statement by placing the number of the appropriate response in the blank space next to the statement.

1	2	3	4	5
Never	Once in a while	Half the time	Often	Very often

_____ 1. The telephone is answered by the third ring.

_____ 2. The person answering the telephone is courteous and friendly.

_____ 3. I am placed on hold for more than 30 seconds.

_____ 4. My call is directed to the appropriate person.

_____ 5. The office (store) is conveniently located and easy to find.

_____ 6. There is ample parking available near the office (store).

_____ 7. The atmosphere of the office (store) is warm and inviting.

_____ 8. The regularly scheduled office (store) hours are convenient for me.

_____ 9. The salesperson or the service provider greets me immediately.

_____ 10. I wait less than 15 minutes if my appointment is delayed.

_____ 11. Prices are appropriate for the products and services provided.

_____ 12. Payment terms for the products or services are flexible.

_____ 13. Payment methods are acceptable.

_____ 14. I receive good value for my money.

_____ 15. The office (store) staff is courteous and friendly.

CUSTOMER SERVICE INVENTORY
(continued)

_____ **16.** The service provider/owner is courteous and friendly.

_____ **17.** I receive personalized attention and service.

_____ **18.** My complaints are resolved quickly and to my satisfaction.

_____ **19.** The service provider and/or staff answers all my questions to my satisfaction.

_____ **20.** The service provider and/or staff is concerned about my situation.

_____ **21.** I am involved in decisions regarding my purchase.

_____ **22.** I feel comfortable with the personality of the service provider (staff).

_____ **23.** I am kept informed of all details regarding my purchase.

_____ **24.** I am happy with the way the service provider (staff) treats me.

_____ **25.** I feel the service provider (staff) is qualified to provide me with these services.

_____ **26.** I prefer to use these services rather than those provided by someone else.

_____ **27.** I can schedule an appointment or shop at the store when it is convenient for me.

_____ **28.** I will use this service provider (store) again.

_____ **29.** I would refer people to this service provider (store).

_____ **30.** The overall quality of the service is high.

Thank you for completing this inventory. Your answers will help us better understand your needs and improve the quality of the services we offer to you.

CUSTOMER SATISFACTION SURVEY

We are interested in finding out how satisfied you are with the services and treatment you received. Please respond to each statement by placing the number of the appropriate response in the blank space next to the statement.

1	2	3	4	5
Extremely dissatisfied	Slightly dissatisfied	Neither satisfied nor dissatisfied	Slightly satisfied	Extremely satisfied

How satisfied are you with:

_____ 1. The location of the office (store)

_____ 2. The parking around the office (store)

_____ 3. The scheduled office (store) hours

_____ 4. The office (store) atmosphere and decor

_____ 5. The telephone manners of the staff

_____ 6. The treatment you receive from the staff

_____ 7. The treatment you receive from the service provider

_____ 8. The prices for the services

_____ 9. The payment methods and terms

_____ 10. The quality of the services

_____ 11. The qualifications of the service provider

_____ 12. The manner in which your complaints are handled

_____ 13. The manner in which your questions are answered

_____ 14. The professionalism of the staff

_____ 15. The marketing and advertising programs of the service provider

A P P E N D I X

B

Customer Information and Profile

The best way to satisfy and retain your customers is to know as much about them as possible. You should know their likes and dislikes, their buying histories, their needs and anything else that will help you seem more personable to them. Your goal is to always maintain their loyalty and retain them as customers.

If you have a customer database, use it. It is your most effective service and marketing tool. If you do not have a computer for your business, the following two forms will help you.

Your customers may complete the classification information form or it can be filled out by your staff, who ask the customers the questions. The customer profile should be filled out by your staff so that all the necessary information is captured on the form. You may adapt the forms to fit your business.

CLASSIFICATION INFORMATION

To learn more about you and to continue providing you with high quality service, we would appreciate it if you would fill in the requested information. Thank you.

Name: _____

Address: _____

City: _____ State: _____ Zip: _____

Telephone: (H) _____ (B) _____

Age: _____ Gender: M _____ F_____

Marital status: Married ___ Single ___ Divorced ___ Widowed ___

Family Size: _____ Occupation: _____

Education Completed: High School _____ Graduate School _____

College _____ Vocational/Trade _____

Date of Last Visit: _____

Household Income: (Check one)

$10,000 – $19,999 _____

$20,000 – $29,999 _____

$30,000 – $39,999 _____

$40,000 – $49,999 _____

$50,000 – $59,999 _____

$60,000 – $69,999 _____

$70,000 + _____

CUSTOMER PROFILE

Name: _____ Telephone: _____

Address: _____

City: _____ State: _____ Zip: _____

Personal Information:

Birthdate: _____ Anniversary: _____

Spouse's Name: _____ Children: _____

Characteristics/Likes/Dislikes: _____

_____

Special Interests/Hobbies: _____

Business Information:

Company Name: _____ Title: _____

Job Anniv. _____ Telephone: _____

Secretary's Name: _____

Reports To: _____ Title: _____ Ext.: _____

Office Contacts: _____

Purchasing Authority: _____ Volume: _____

Purchase Habits/Preferences: _____

Currently Buys From: _____

Satisfaction Level: _____

Needs/Benefits/Solutions:

Current Needs: _____

Future Needs: _____

Current Problems: _____

Benefits/Solutions: _____

Call Date: _____ Response: _____

Next Call: _____ Action: _____

NOTES

NOTES

NOTES

NOTES

NOTES

NOTES

NOTES

NOTES

NOTES

NOTES

NOTES

NOTES

Also Available

Subject Areas Include:

Accounting & Finance

Business Ethics

Business Skills

Communication

Customer Service

Design

Diversity in Business

Human Resources & Leveraging Your People

Jobs & Careers

Management & Leadership

Operations

Product Development & Marketing

Sales Coaching & Prospecting

Women in Leadership

Writing & Editing

AX1560524618
ISBN-13 978-1-56052-461-8
ISBN-10 1-56052-461-8

9 781560 524618